In this volume, the authors chart the histories of their lives as feminists in the world of higher education. And as they do so, they inevitably approach the issue of institutional reform. No consensus is reached on the manner or extent of desirable reform, and though these women of dissimilar backgrounds and personalities agree on much, they make no attempt to disguise their differences.

All the authors, however, are torn between their awareness of "the formidable power of male-conceived and male-controlled law" and their intense desire to see feminism "overthrow that empire—not in exchange for an equally oppressive matriarchy, but rather to achieve the equalization of power." Whether one shares that desire or not, one can admire the authors' energy and sensitivity as they show us how the present educational system obstructs the equalization of power and in what ways the system must change in order to foster it.

Florence Howe, the editor of *Women and the Power to Change*, is professor of humanities at State University of New York, College at Old Westbury.

Carnegie Commission on Higher Education
Sponsored Research Studies

THE NEW DEPRESSION IN HIGHER
EDUCATION:
A STUDY OF FINANCIAL CONDITIONS AT 41
COLLEGES AND UNIVERSITIES
Earl F. Cheit

FINANCING MEDICAL EDUCATION:
AN ANALYSIS OF ALTERNATIVE POLICIES
AND MECHANISMS
Rashi Fein and
Gerald I. Weber

HIGHER EDUCATION IN NINE COUNTRIES:
A COMPARATIVE STUDY OF COLLEGES AND
UNIVERSITIES ABROAD
Barbara B. Burn, Philip G. Altbach, Clark Kerr,
and James A. Perkins

BRIDGES TO UNDERSTANDING:
INTERNATIONAL PROGRAMS OF AMERICAN
COLLEGES AND UNIVERSITIES
Irwin T. Sanders and
Jennifer C. Ward

GRADUATE AND PROFESSIONAL EDUCATION,
1980:
A SURVEY OF INSTITUTIONAL PLANS
Lewis B. Mayhew
(Out of print, but available from University Micro-
films.)

THE AMERICAN COLLEGE AND AMERICAN
CULTURE:
SOCIALIZATION AS A FUNCTION OF HIGHER
EDUCATION
Oscar Handlin and
Mary F. Handlin

RECENT ALUMNI AND HIGHER EDUCATION:
A SURVEY OF COLLEGE GRADUATES
Joe L. Spaeth and Andrew M. Greeley
(Out of print, but available from University Micro-
films.)

CHANGE IN EDUCATIONAL POLICY:
SELF-STUDIES IN SELECTED COLLEGES AND
UNIVERSITIES
Dwight R. Ladd

STATE OFFICIALS AND HIGHER EDUCATION:
A SURVEY OF THE OPINIONS AND EXPECTA-
TIONS OF POLICY MAKERS IN NINE STATES
Heinz Eulau and Harold Quinley
(Out of print, but available from University Micro-
films.)

ACADEMIC DEGREE STRUCTURES, INNOVATIVE
APPROACHES:
PRINCIPLES OF REFORM IN DEGREE
STRUCTURES IN THE
UNITED STATES
Stephen H. Spurr

COLLEGES OF THE FORGOTTEN AMERICANS:
A PROFILE OF STATE COLLEGES AND REGIONAL
UNIVERSITIES
E. Alden Dunham

FROM BACKWATER TO MAINSTREAM:
A PROFILE OF CATHOLIC HIGHER
EDUCATION
Andrew M. Greeley

THE ECONOMICS OF THE MAJOR PRIVATE
UNIVERSITIES
William G. Bowen
(Out of print, but available from University Micro-
films.)

THE FINANCE OF HIGHER EDUCATION
Howard R. Bowen
(Out of print, but available from University Micro-
films.)

ALTERNATIVE METHODS OF FEDERAL FUNDING
FOR HIGHER EDUCATION
Ron Wolk
(Out of print, but available from University Micro-
films.)

INVENTORY OF CURRENT RESEARCH ON
HIGHER EDUCATION 1968
Dale M. Heckman and
Warren Bryan Martin
(Out of print, but available from University Micro-
films.)

The following technical reports are available from the Carnegie Commission on Higher Education, 2150 Shattuck Ave., Berkeley, California 94704.

RESOURCE USE IN HIGHER EDUCATION:
TRENDS IN OUTPUT AND INPUTS, 1930–1967
June O'Neill

TRENDS AND PROJECTIONS OF PHYSICIANS IN
THE UNITED STATES 1967–2002
Mark S. Blumberg

MAY 1970:
THE CAMPUS AFTERMATH OF CAMBODIA AND
KENT STATE
Richard E. Peterson and John A. Bilorusky

MENTAL ABILITY AND HIGHER EDUCATIONAL
ATTAINMENT IN THE 20TH CENTURY
Paul Taubman and Terence Wales

AMERICAN COLLEGE AND UNIVERSITY
ENROLLMENT TRENDS IN 1971
Richard E. Peterson

PAPERS ON EFFICIENCY IN THE MANAGEMENT
OF HIGHER EDUCATION
*Alexander M. Mood, Colin Bell, Lawrence
Bogard, Helen Brownlee, and Joseph McCloskey*

AN INVENTORY OF ACADEMIC INNOVATION
AND REFORM
Ann Heiss

ESTIMATING THE RETURNS TO EDUCATION:
A DISAGGREGATED APPROACH
Richard S. Eckaus

SOURCES OF FUNDS TO COLLEGES AND
UNIVERSITIES
June O'Neill

NEW DEPRESSION IN HIGHER EDUCATION—
TWO YEARS LATER
Earl F. Cheit

PROFESSORS, UNIONS, AND AMERICAN
HIGHER EDUCATION
*Everett Carll Ladd, Jr. and Seymour Martin
Lipset*

A CLASSIFICATION OF INSTITUTIONS OF
HIGHER EDUCATION

POLITICAL IDEOLOGIES OF GRADUATE
STUDENTS:
CRYSTALLIZATION, CONSISTENCY, AND
CONTEXTUAL EFFECT
*Margaret Fay and
Jeff Weintraub*

FLYING A LEARNING CENTER:
DESIGN AND COSTS OF AN OFF-CAMPUS SPACE
FOR LEARNING
Thomas J. Karwin

THE DEMISE OF DIVERSITY?:
A COMPARATIVE PROFILE OF EIGHT TYPES OF
INSTITUTIONS
C. Robert Pace

TUITION:
A SUPPLEMENTAL STATEMENT TO THE REPORT
OF THE CARNEGIE COMMISSION ON HIGHER
EDUCATION ON "WHO PAYS? WHO BENEFITS?
WHO SHOULD PAY?"

THE GREAT AMERICAN DEGREE MACHINE
Douglas L. Adkins

The following reprints are available from the Carnegie Commission on Higher Education, 2150 Shattuck Ave., Berkeley, California 94704.

ACCELERATED PROGRAMS OF MEDICAL EDUCATION, *by Mark S. Blumberg, reprinted from*
JOURNAL OF MEDICAL EDUCATION, *vol. 46, no. 8, August 1971.**

SCIENTIFIC MANPOWER FOR 1970–1985, *by Allan M. Cartter, reprinted from* SCIENCE, *vol. 172,
no. 3979, pp. 132–140, April 9, 1971.*

*The Commission's stock of this reprint has been exhausted.

A NEW METHOD OF MEASURING STATES' HIGHER EDUCATION BURDEN, *by Neil Timm, reprinted from* THE JOURNAL OF HIGHER EDUCATION, *vol. 42, no. 1, pp. 27–33, January 1971.* *

REGENT WATCHING, *by Earl F. Cheit, reprinted from* AGB REPORTS, *vol. 13, no. 6, pp. 4–13, March 1971.* *

COLLEGE GENERATIONS—FROM THE 1930S TO THE 1960S, *by Seymour M. Lipset and Everett C. Ladd, Jr., reprinted from* THE PUBLIC INTEREST, *no. 25, Summer 1971.*

AMERICAN SOCIAL SCIENTISTS AND THE GROWTH OF CAMPUS POLITICAL ACTIVISM IN THE 1960S, *by Everett C. Ladd, Jr., and Seymour M. Lipset, reprinted from* SOCIAL SCIENCES INFORMATION, *Vol. 10, no. 2, April 1971.*

THE POLITICS OF AMERICAN POLITICAL SCIENTISTS, *by Everett C. Ladd, Jr., and Seymour M. Lipset, reprinted from* PS, *vol. 4, no. 2, Spring 1971.* *

THE DIVIDED PROFESSORIATE, *by Seymour M. Lipset and Everett C. Ladd, Jr., reprinted from* CHANGE, *vol. 3, no. 3, pp. 54–60, May 1971.* *

JEWISH ACADEMICS IN THE UNITED STATES: THEIR ACHIEVEMENTS, CULTURE AND POLITICS, *by Seymour M. Lipset and Everett C. Ladd, Jr., reprinted from* AMERICAN JEWISH YEAR BOOK, *1971.*

THE UNHOLY ALLIANCE AGAINST THE CAMPUS, *by Kenneth Keniston and Michael Lerner, reprinted from* NEW YORK TIMES MAGAZINE, *November 8, 1970.*

PRECARIOUS PROFESSORS: NEW PATTERNS OF REPRESENTATION, *by Joseph W. Garbarino, reprinted from* INDUSTRIAL RELATIONS, *vol. 10, no. 1, February 1971.* *

. . . AND WHAT PROFESSORS THINK: ABOUT STUDENT PROTEST AND MANNERS, MORALS, POLITICS, AND CHAOS ON THE CAMPUS, *by Seymour Martin Lipset and Everett C. Ladd, Jr., reprinted from* PSYCHOLOGY TODAY, *November 1970.* *

DEMAND AND SUPPLY IN U.S. HIGHER EDUCATION: A PROGRESS REPORT, *by Roy Radner and Leonard S. Miller, reprinted from* AMERICAN ECONOMIC REVIEW, *May 1970.* *

RESOURCES FOR HIGHER EDUCATION: AN ECONOMIST'S VIEW, *by Theodore W. Schultz, reprinted from* JOURNAL OF POLITICAL ECONOMY, *vol. 76, no. 3, University of Chicago, May/June 1968.* *

INDUSTRIAL RELATIONS AND UNIVERSITY RELATIONS, *by Clark Kerr, reprinted from* PROCEEDINGS OF THE 21ST ANNUAL WINTER MEETING OF THE INDUSTRIAL RELATIONS RESEARCH ASSOCIATION, *pp. 15–25.* *

NEW CHALLENGES TO THE COLLEGE AND UNIVERSITY, *by Clark Kerr, reprinted from Kermit Gordon (ed.),* AGENDA FOR THE NATION, *The Brookings Institution, Washington, D.C., 1968.* *

PRESIDENTIAL DISCONTENT, *by Clark Kerr, reprinted from David C. Nichols (ed.),* PERSPEC-

The Commission's stock of this reprint has been exhausted.

TIVES ON CAMPUS TENSIONS: PAPERS PREPARED FOR THE SPECIAL COMMITTEE ON CAMPUS TENSIONS, *American Council on Education, Washington, D.C., September 1970.**

STUDENT PROTEST—AN INSTITUTIONAL AND NATIONAL PROFILE, *by Harold Hodgkinson, reprinted from* THE RECORD, *vol. 71, no. 4, May 1970.**

WHAT'S BUGGING THE STUDENTS?, *by Kenneth Keniston, reprinted from* EDUCATIONAL RECORD, *American Council on Education, Washington, D.C., Spring 1970.**

THE POLITICS OF ACADEMIA, *by Seymour Martin Lipset, reprinted from David C. Nichols (ed.),* PERSPECTIVES ON CAMPUS TENSIONS: PAPERS PREPARED FOR THE SPECIAL COMMITTEE ON CAMPUS TENSIONS, *American Council on Education, Washington, D.C., September 1970.**

INTERNATIONAL PROGRAMS OF U.S. COLLEGES AND UNIVERSITIES: PRIORITIES FOR THE SEVENTIES, *by James A. Perkins, reprinted by permission of the International Council for Educational Development, Occasional Paper no. 1, July 1971.*

FACULTY UNIONISM: FROM THEORY TO PRACTICE, *by Joseph W. Garbarino, reprinted from* INDUSTRIAL RELATIONS, *vol. 11, no. 1, pp. 1–17, February 1972.*

MORE FOR LESS: HIGHER EDUCATION'S NEW PRIORITY, *by Virginia B. Smith, reprinted from* UNIVERSAL HIGHER EDUCATION: COSTS AND BENEFITS, *American Council on Education, Washington, D.C., 1971.*

ACADEMIA AND POLITICS IN AMERICA, *by Seymour M. Lipset, reprinted from Thomas I. Nossiter (ed.),* IMAGINATION AND PRECISION IN THE SOCIAL SCIENCES, *pp. 211–289, Faber and Faber, London, 1972.*

POLITICS OF ACADEMIC NATURAL SCIENTISTS AND ENGINEERS, *by Everett C. Ladd, Jr., and Seymour M. Lipset, reprinted from* SCIENCE, *vol. 176, no. 4039, pp. 1091–1100, June 9, 1972.*

THE INTELLECTUAL AS CRITIC AND REBEL, WITH SPECIAL REFERENCE TO THE UNITED STATES AND THE SOVIET UNION, *by Seymour M. Lipset and Richard B. Dobson, reprinted from* DAEDALUS, *vol. 101, no. 3, pp. 137–198, Summer 1972.*

THE POLITICS OF AMERICAN SOCIOLOGISTS, *by Seymour M. Lipset and Everett C. Ladd, Jr., reprinted from* THE AMERICAN JOURNAL OF SOCIOLOGY, *vol. 78, no. 1, July 1972.*

THE DISTRIBUTION OF ACADEMIC TENURE IN AMERICAN HIGHER EDUCATION, *by Martin Trow, reprinted from* THE TENURE DEBATE, *Bardwell Smith (ed.), Jossey-Bass, San Francisco, 1972.*

THE NATURE AND ORIGINS OF THE CARNEGIE COMMISSION ON HIGHER EDUCATION, *by Alan Pifer, based on a speech delivered to the Pennsylvania Association of Colleges and Universities, Oct. 16, 1972, reprinted by permission of the Carnegie Foundation for the Advancement of Teaching.*

*The Commission's stock of this reprint has been exhausted.

COMING OF MIDDLE AGE IN HIGHER EDUCATION, *by Earl F. Cheit, address delivered to American Association of State Colleges and Universities and National Association of State Universities and Land-Grant Colleges, Nov. 13, 1972.*

MEASURING FACULTY UNIONISM: QUANTITY AND QUALITY, *by Bill Aussieker and J. W. Garbarino, reprinted from* INDUSTRIAL RELATIONS, *vol. 12, no. 2, May 1973.*

PROBLEMS IN THE TRANSITION FROM ELITE TO MASS HIGHER EDUCATION, *by Martin Trow, paper prepared for a conference on mass higher education sponsored by the Organization for Economic Co-operation and Development, June 1973.*

*Women and
the Power to Change*

Women and the Power to Change

edited by *Florence Howe*

Professor of Humanities
State University of New York
College at Old Westbury

A Volume of Essays Sponsored by
The Carnegie Commission on Higher Education

MC GRAW-HILL BOOK COMPANY

New York   St. Louis   San Francisco
Düsseldorf   Johannesburg   Kuala Lumpur   London   Mexico
Montreal   New Delhi   Panama   Paris   São Paulo
Singapore   Sydney   Tokyo   Toronto

The Carnegie Commission on Higher Education
2150 Shattuck Avenue, Berkeley, California 94704
has sponsored preparation of this report as part
of a continuing effort to obtain and present
significant information for public discussion.
The views expressed are those of the authors.

WOMEN AND THE POWER TO CHANGE

This book was set in Palatino by Black Dot Computer Typesetting
Corp. It was printed and bound by The Maple Press Company.
The designer was Elliot Epstein. The editors were
Nancy Tressel and Janine Parson for McGraw-Hill Book Company
and Verne A. Stadtman and Karen Seriguchi for the
Carnegie Commission on Higher Education. Audre Hanneman
edited the index. Milton J. Heiberg supervised the production.

Library of Congress Cataloging in Publication Data

Main entry under title:

Women and the power to change.

"Essays sponsored by the Carnegie Commission on
Higher Education."
Includes bibliographies.
1. Higher education of women—United States—
Addresses, essays, lectures. 2. Women's rights—United
States—Addresses, essays, lectures. I. Howe,
Florence, ed. II. Carnegie Commission on Higher
Education.
LC1756.W657   378   74-17374
ISBN 0-07-010124-8

1 2 3 4 5 6 7 8 9 MAMM 7 9 8 7 6 5

Contents

Contributors

Arlie Hochschild
Assistant Professor of Sociology
University of California, Berkeley

Florence Howe
Professor of Humanities
State University of New York,
*   College at Old Westbury*

Adrienne Rich
Professor of English
City University of New York,
*   City College*

Aleta Wallach
Member of the California bar

Foreword

The male-oriented bias of the traditional university in this country has been well documented in recent literature. The Carnegie Commission, for example, studied the situation of academic women in its report *Opportunities for Women in Higher Education,* and the findings can leave no doubt that grave sex-based inequalities do exist. And in the Commission-sponsored report *Escape from the Doll's House,* Saul D. Feldman documents the historical and present-day attitudes that have seriously hindered women in their efforts to achieve equal educational opportunity.

Behind the historical and statistical records lie the struggles of individual women to reconcile their desires to succeed with their knowledge of a society whose rules were made, as Arlie Hochschild put it, for "the traditional man with his traditional wife." This book is a collection of four personal accounts of that struggle—out of which have also come visions for a future in which such struggles will no longer have to take place. The visions of institutional and social reform contained in this volume may seem utopian to some. I would agree with its editor, however, that to admit the possibility of change "is to take the first step to its achievement," and by suggesting some changes for our consideration, the authors have made interesting and challenging contributions to such progress.

Clark Kerr

Chairman
Carnegie Commission
on Higher Education

May 1975

*Women and
the Power to Change*

Introduction

by Florence Howe

This book was to have been rapidly produced a year ago: a series of essays on the lives of women in academe some four or five years after the women's movement had begun to make its mark on campuses. But it did not work out that way. The writing of this book illustrates one significant aspect of the lives of academic women: overcommitment. I speak chiefly, but not only, for myself here, as I describe my life. The book had to be written and edited during the interstices of weeks filled with teaching, meetings, lectures, consultations, correspondence: with developing, coordinating, and teaching in a women's studies program; developing a second women's studies program for public school teachers; coordinating The Feminist Press, a sizable educational and publishing enterprise; corresponding with countless women who would like to study, begin research about, teach in, or produce materials or films for women's studies. In addition, academic women these days are in demand as consultants to governmental agencies, university administrations, textbook publishers, and legislators; or as participants in conferences as panelists, and especially as lecturers on college campuses anxious to give their students a look at a "new woman." In short, the retiring or invisible woman in academe has been replaced by a person too busy for her own life. Indeed, she may have little life beyond her work.

Thus far at least, the chief effect of the women's movement on higher education has been as I have described it above: an impact on the lives of academic women, including students. While the movement has reached thousands of students, chiefly through women's studies courses and programs, it has not yet begun the task of changing institutions themselves. The four of us who came together to write this book have felt our individual lives

1

change these past four or five years, and part of this book records some of those changes.

The agent of that change was feminism, first as consciousness, then as ideology. Through different experiences, and at different points in our lives, we came to see the world as unfriendly or inimical to women. Perhaps we were, at the time, the singular woman poet, the academic woman named to high office in a professional association, the only woman professor in a college sociology department, or one of very few women accepted into a law school class. Our singular positions operated not only to distinguish us, but to force us to consider that singularity. Were we "special" or merely fortunate? What had we done (and what would we have to do) to get (and maintain) our positions in what was, we were beginning to perceive, a man's world? Who or what controlled our behavior and ideas? In our positions as tokens, how did we relate to men, and how to women?

The answers to those and other questions, systematically organized, moved us from consciousness to ideology—to discovering, as C. Wright Mills has put it, the link between "public issues and private troubles." We understood that not accident but historical forces and institutionalized patriarchy accounted for our "places" as token women. Each of us separately, in the years before we came together to write this book, had become feminists interested in institutional change. The force of our ideology led us in that direction. Each of us separately, long before we knew each other, had been instrumental in some organization of academic women, either on a campus or in a professional association, pressing either for new women's studies courses or for child care or other institutional changes beneficial to women.

This book, then, represents an attempt to chart both the changing lives and thoughts of four academic women and the new ideology that informs those lives—informs, but does not necessarily integrate. For academic women, feminism raises more problems and conflicts than it currently offers solutions. Are we working to promote a few women to high academic office, one might challenge? Or even a large number of women? Or are we interested in opening the gates of academe to all women, and in a manner not possible on campuses today? Are we prescribing separate educational facilities and opportunities for women? Or are we interested in changing the conditions under which all people gain access to and study in the university?

Though we may agree on much, the authors of this volume have done nothing to disguise our differences or to pose solutions for problems we are only now learning to name.

THE WRITERS We are hardly, in any ultimate sense, "representative" academic women. Two of us are in our mid-forties, the other two twenty-eight and thirty-three, respectively. Two of us are married, one widowed, one single: two are mothers, two are not. Only one of us holds the Ph.D., another the doctor of jurisprudence, a third the B.A., and I am an M.A. with years of graduate work minus the doctoral dissertation. Arlie Hochschild and I have been academics throughout our lives; she in sociology for some six years, I for more than twenty, mainly in literature and writing but now in women's studies and education as well. As a law student, young attorney Aleta Wallach taught courses in Women and the Law; Adrienne Rich has taught writing and literature on several campuses during the past decade of her life, but she is primarily a poet.

What unites us? That we were known to each other through our writing at least, for we had already published on feminism as activists and intellectuals in the academic women's movement. That we were committed to institutional change on campus. That we are white and lead middle-class lives tells you something about the university and the women's movement both. What we have to say represents a spectrum of opinion confined to our diverse lives and experiences. Quite another book might be written by black academic women for whom sexism is a second barrier. And another book still by other minority women— Puerto Ricans, Chicanas, Asians, and native Americans—for whom the dual burden of racism and sexism is harder even than it is for black women.

Quite another book might be written also by women younger or older than we; by lesbian women; by women in "harder" disciplines; by women less "successful" or more "successful." While one of us has had a very difficult time finding a teaching job, another of us teaches at one of the most prestigious institutions in the country. None of us teaches at a private institution, and only one of us regularly teaches graduate students. We are full professors and assistants, at the start or in the middle of academic careers.

What unites us also is a commitment to the university as a

workplace, in part because we enjoy and value teaching, in part because we are interested in the discovery of strategic knowledge. And so, this is not a book that attempts simply to disparage the university either as a place to work or as a corrupt center of power. Adrienne Rich and Aleta Wallach, who as poet and lawyer, respectively, may feel more distant from the university than Arlie Hochschild or I, write passionately of the university as "a breeding ground of masculine privilege" and "a transmitter of social values and class interests hostile to women." Yet we should also agree with Rich that "we need the university, with its libraries, laboratories, archives, collections, and some—but not all—of the kinds of trained thinking and expertise it has to offer."

We need the university also because it is a powerful lever in the larger society. Few feminists this past decade have been willing to think or talk of power. Perhaps it was utopian to consider that a straggling band of women, on or off campus, could grow strong enough to effect institutional change through the use of power. Obviously, we have not done so yet. But we are only at the beginning of another century of effort, and as in the past century, one prime target is higher education for women.

THE UNIVERSITY Aleta Wallach was a first-year law school student at the start of the women's movement on campus; Arlie Hochschild was a Berkeley student at the start of the student movement in the mid-sixties. Only Adrienne Rich and I remember what it was like to be a woman student in the late forties—she at Radcliffe, I at Hunter. Bright women even at women's colleges learned to think as the ubiquitous generic "man," and never to consider their histories as women. We identified with Pip and scorned or pitied Estella; we spent most of our time listening to teachers lecture about the dilemmas of great tragic heroes—the parade of Oedipus, Lear, Macbeth, and Hamlet, or, on occasion, a contemporary male out of Anderson or Miller. We learned to write with the models of the great male poets and prose writers before us: Blake, Wordsworth, Keats, Emerson, and Thoreau, and perhaps more daringly, Yeats and Eliot. If we wanted to succeed, we should have to be like *them;* and yet—this was unspoken and unthought except in dreams—how could *we* be like *them?*

Though I was fortunate enough to have had excellent women teachers, at Radcliffe Adrienne Rich had none. On one particular occasion, moreover, she was excluded by two professors from a seminar on Joyce's *Finnegan's Wake* because it was deemed impossible to deal with the sexual materials of the novel in mixed company. Despite such differences in our experiences, we both describe our special opportunities for achievement as due to the interest of particularly powerful "great" men, a poet in one case, a college president in another. But our success as students translated itself into lives appropriate only for women: one took the path of marriage and mothering, with poetry on the side; the other the path of marriage and divorce, with teaching on the side. For neither of us believed that we could make a life for ourselves in or out of the university without first fulfilling our responsibility to be wives and mothers. Our lives as working people, our creative work lives, had at best to take second place. Neither of us could have eschewed marriage and motherhood, nor could we have envisioned a truly egalitarian marriage in which our own work mattered as much as our husbands'. And only in the fourth decade of our lives did we—separately and under different circumstances—reach other conclusions. The watershed of our lives, not surprisingly, was also a significant turning point for the university.

Only children under 12 in our schools today cannot remember the sit-ins, marches, and mass demonstrations that flickered across the TV screen alternately with images of burning Vietnamese peasants and children and grim-faced young soldiers on both sides. It is always difficult to write the history of one's own time, but I venture to guess that no single event has so pushed the world onto the campus as the Vietnamese war. There was a connection, faculty and students learned, between the campus and the ability of a government to carry on a war; there were also professors and other campus officials both for and against the war—with relative degrees of responsibility and influence in the nation. Whatever the future impact of the sixties on higher education, for many of us the decade ended the illusion of the university as an institution isolated from the mainstream of national power. The university is government's vital resource, not only for research but for personnel; the movement of information and Kissingers from campus to state department has been elaborately documented.

The activism of the sixties did not begin with the war, but with the civil rights movement. Three responses of the campus to the pressures for minority representation have had wide-reaching effects: a broadening of curricular offerings; open admissions; and the special recruitment of minority faculty and administrators, a precedent to formal affirmative action programs. The attempt to bring minority (particularly black) students onto large Northern campuses was accompanied by a growing tendency for those minority populations to segregate themselves either socially or culturally or in black studies departments. That trend has continued, in part because, as Nathan Hare has said, separatism is "therapeutic" and hence necessary, even as a preliminary to "integration"; but it may be also that separatism becomes too comfortable to alter easily.

As the war was in its last and most destructive phases toward the close of the sixties, a few women on campuses began to document the status of women faculty or to initiate the first women's studies courses. Though academic women have learned a great deal from academic blacks and other minority groups, and though they are these days often pitted against each other as applicants for posts and as targets of affirmative action policies, their status is essentially distinct. For women are not a minority but a majority of the population. On campuses, white women have been at least moderately represented for nearly a hundred years, and currently they are more than 40 percent of the student population. While the recruitment of women undergraduates is not an issue, the curriculum and facilities for women are. On the other hand, a very much smaller percentage of women than men choose to go on to graduate or professional school, and a still smaller proportion than men complete their training. As faculty and administrators, women are underrepresented in proportion both to the student body and to the number of those eligible in their respective fields; where they are employed, moreover, they are typically in the lower ranks, or at nonprestigious institutions, or among the part-time personnel. Only in the ranks of clerical employees are women more than adequately represented, and here there are other issues: janitorial and cleaners' jobs, for example, are likely to be ranked above typists' and stenographers', and paid accordingly. Thus, the issues for women are divided between recruitment and inequities.

On campuses, these issues have been translated into two major efforts: changing the curriculum; and encouraging the employment, promotion, and tenure of academic women or their recruitment into administrative posts. Both of these have raised critical questions about merit and separatism.

As a group, the writers of this volume are probably more in accord on the issue of merit than on separatism. Charges have come from certain quarters of the male academy that to support the hiring or promotion of women or members of minorities is to lower the standards of the academic profession and thus to destroy the meritocracy on which the university has been built. The assumptions are dual: that women and members of minorities are as a class inferior to white males; and, second, that the university normally functions as a meritocracy. If such charges have not received adequate response thus far from academic women, it is that the latter undoubtedly strikes them as absurd, the former as insulting. No civil service examinations or "professorial record exams" rank academics in consequent order. No legitimate "list" exists that might conceivably make credible a "merit" system of recruitment, appointment, reappointment, promotion, and tenure. Instead, young graduate students learn quickly that another, wholly nonmeritocratic process directs their future: the crucial choice of a prestigious Ph.D.-granting institution; the equally crucial choice of a professor—with connections and the willingness to "place" his students in their first critical job. That process under way, the rest depends on the young Ph.D.'s ability, not simply or only to publish quickly, but more important by far, to "get along" with those in power in his new department. This process, again, is hardly a meritocratic one, but, as Arlie Hochschild indicates, is dependent upon a series of assumptions and expectations about his maleness as well as his working style. It is better, for example, to do committee work unobtrusively and without creating department disturbances by raising questions of either procedure or direction; it is better to be a staid, scholarly, and thus "responsible" teacher with modest enrollments than a huge success, since popularity with students can be interpreted as sinister—you are too "easy," or you are "catering" to students' interests.

Assuming the inferiority of women as a group is, of course, still current, though only extremists will state the axiom forthrightly. As we know, such thinking also allows the occasional woman or minority-group member to succeed as the "exception." Thus, some academic women and members of minorities currently in the profession may fall into the exceptional category, though most are at the bottom of the profession's hierarchy. On the other hand, one can point to recent studies by Helen Astin and others that document the work histories of academic women (including minority women): their superior school and college records; their stability as employees—reflecting their loyalty to institutions; their commitment to teaching as more significant than research; and their remarkable research and publishing records despite heavier teaching loads than males. Despite the excellence, even occasionally the superiority, of these women, the same studies indicate that merit is hardly their reward. Women are paid less, hold lower ranks, and are promoted more slowly than men, even where the credentials of the males are clearly inferior to those of the females. Indeed, studies of the achievement of academic women provide data for a detailed indictment of university meritocracy.

The issue of separatism is, in some respects, intertwined with the issue of merit. The studies of the university as nonmeritocratic have led women to consider separatism as an alternative. If equity is impossible to achieve, even in a decade or two, much less "with all deliberate speed," then what women need may be wholly feminist institutions. It is not simply impatience: it is also a strategy for change as old and well-used as any other. If you cannot change an institution either quickly enough or well enough, then found your own to do the job: it is the history of higher education for women and minority groups in the United States. As such, however, separatism has its limitations, its chief one the avoidance or postponement of confrontation on the essential issues of inferiority/superiority. Women's colleges, for example, created their own hierarchy, but even the best of those institutions existed quite separately from, and at the bottom of, the hierarchies of excellent male *and* coeducational institutions. I would not argue that, theoretically, all separatism is useless, but at this moment, I doubt that new institutional separatism would be either therapeutic or strategically beneficial to women.

On campuses the issues of merit and separatism appear palpably in the (usually quite separate) establishment of affirmative action offices and women's studies programs or "centers." Offices, personnel, style, and strategy are not only distinctive; they are often antagonistic. The source of the antagonism is obvious enough. Women's studies is a grass roots movement, mainly of young graduate students and undergraduates and young, nontenured faculty. It has developed without official administrative sanction, and occasionally despite departmental hostility. On most campuses still, it operates as an "underground" academic enterprise, without the legitimacy of tenured faculty and generous budgets or large offices. Affirmative action has come to all campuses officially at the behest of federal mandates, albeit the pressures were originally grass roots ones. Usually, the affirmative action officer (who may or may not be a woman) is hired by the highest administrators of the institution and must necessarily work at least in close proximity to them. Often, the job as conceived on particular campuses calls for administrative experience, and the person chosen must reflect the administrative style of the institution, rather than its academic ambiance. Obviously, posts are being filled by women (and men) who have had no former connection with the earlier grass roots movements of women on university campuses. The official status of affirmative action officers—as well as the nature of their jobs—tends therefore to separate them from those faculty and students engaged in women's studies, despite the fact that one might conceive that affirmative action hiring would lead to the strengthening of women's (and black and other minority) studies on campuses.

New institutional forms of separatism on campuses are the women's studies programs and the women's centers that have accompanied or substituted for them. Increasingly, these have been supported or at least sanctioned by the university, as though there were some agreement—unspoken, of course—that it is currently simpler to give up some turf both to women and to minority groups rather than to respond to the pressures for universitywide reexamination and revision. I am genuinely concerned that women and minority groups will rest content with their piece of turf rather than turn their energetic movements into strategies for changing the university as a whole.

The current pressures from academic women come to the university as it attempts to recover from the civil rights, antiwar, and student power upheavals of the sixties; as it attempts to "retrench" amid a failing economy and an expected decline in student population; and as it continues a general if slow shift of energy, numbers, even excellence, from elite private institutions to mass-based statewide systems. In one sense, the women's movement is a decade late: women missed the opportunity for upward mobility through the sixties that male academics, now in positions of power, then seized. What crumbs remain—affirmative action posts, for example—are thrown out to be fought over by women and minority males. We are now in a period of reassessment; the decades ahead may be more grim still. But on the other hand, those same factors—a period of relative calm on campuses, of belt tightening, and of a shift in the academic centers of power—may have important consequences for women.

First, the allegedly quiet campus. Wherever I have gone these past three years, on approximately 35 to 40 visits to campuses, their centers of activity have been feminist. Not only have there been efforts to wring child-care facilities from the university, but other kinds of space as well: for "centers" of relaxation, counseling, and research; for women's studies programs, offices, and libraries. On a few campuses women have sat-in for their demands—or organized antirape guerilla actions—and made no headlines in the process. Art, dance, poetry, film, and theatre festivals on campuses have been dominated these past several years by women, and so have conferences and lecture schedules. Indeed, women seem to have filled the space left vacant by those activists of the sixties, and yet, because their style is hardly similar, the campus is reportedly "quiet."

As the young student population stabilizes, the older population that has already begun to demonstrate its interest in "continuing" education is expected to rise. This population thus far has been predominantly female. Studies of its habits and aspirations are just under way. In my experience during the past three years, not only have continuing education and extension programs proliferated even more rapidly than women's studies programs, they have become markedly feminist in character, their course offerings often interchangeable with women's studies. On some campuses, the two programs are cooperative ones.

It is hardly surprising that the largest women's studies programs and continuing education programs are not to be found on elite private campuses. That is not where most of the women faculty or students can be found. They are usually also not to be found on the campuses of the top ten universities, but rather on public college campuses—California State University/Sacramento, Portland State University, or SUNY/Buffalo, for example, where there are more women faculty and fewer upper-class and upper-middle-class students. In the California system, which is to be remarked for its general support of women's programs of all sorts, Berkeley followed some three years behind San Francisco and Sacramento, and to establish its women's center, "stole" key women faculty from both of these less elite institutions.

THE BOOK We begin from two assumptions about the university, one of which is by now a commonplace, the other of which will most certainly become one. In a technological society, the university is a crucially central institution. It controls both knowledge and power through the education and assignment (channeling) of people who flow through its pipelines. Countless studies since the late fifties have demonstrated the interconnections among personnel in universities, industry, and government. More recently, studies have focused on the second assumption from which we begin: the university is a male enclave that allows women to function only in closely restricted areas.

Adrienne Rich reviews the traditional male-centered nature and bias of the university and offers thereby a holistic approach to the issues surrounding women in higher education. Can so damaged an institution serve "the humanism and freedom it professes"? Rich reminds us of Virginia Woolf's query in *Three Guineas:* "Where is it leading us, the procession of educated men?" And her response challenges the traditional direction: in Rich's view, we must move inside the university, as we are already moving outside it, to re-create a feminist history and culture and to serve the needs and interests of women. Women's education is undermined both by the curriculum and by the male-topped hierarchy superimposed on the fragmented lives of women who serve in subordinate positions. Rich recommends both revisions in the curriculum and several institutional reforms, chiefly university-supported child care and arrangements for part-time study and work. She envisions a university sweepingly transformed by its consideration for women: such an institution would refocus not only its course of study and organizational structures, but its research goals and services, so as to be of value to a population of women currently ignored.

While Adrienne Rich scans the university cinematically, Arlie Hochschild closes in to examine the career patterns and daily lives of its faculty. Building on personal experience at Berkeley and Santa Cruz, as well as on the research efforts of the last decade, Hochschild attempts an explanation for the paucity of women in high academic places. Hochschild examines first the two most common and most verified explanations: discrimination, and the socialization of women to avoid "success" and authority. While these patterns do exist, a third pattern, more massive even than they, controls the lives of university people, especially women. In her words, "the classic profile of the academic career is cut to the image of the traditional man with his traditional wife." Hence, even if the meritocracy the university claims to be were made to work in relation to women—through checks on discrimination and the encouragement of women's aspirations—radical inequities would persist. For the university is organized around the employment of males with supportive families—wives who type manuscripts and children who are taught to stay out of father's way. Hochschild's solutions, like Rich's, suggest the necessity for institutional change.

While Rich speculates about the willingness of academic men to *risk* supporting a feminist movement to change the university, neither she nor Hochschild addresses the question of power directly. Their essays focus on change—experienced in the present or envisioned as essential to the future. In the second pair of essays, Aleta Wallach and I, from different points of departure and with somewhat different conclusions, approach the question of power.

As an attorney, Aleta Wallach focuses on her own law school experiences and on her conception of law as "the source of all power, indeed as power itself, conferring or withholding status as it does." As she traces women's presence in and absence from legal training and practice, Wallach builds a case for law as the "rule of men." Males, not the "law," created a world in which women were never intended to share power. Males used the "law" to confer "upon women inferior status and upon men preeminent status." Through its curriculum, admissions policies, and institutional style, the law school became one essential tool for this end.

As one of a handful of pioneers, Wallach describes the recent yielding of the law school to feminists' demands for the admission of more women students and faculty and the revision of curriculum. While she is not optimistic about the long-range effects of feminists' presence in the law school, she sees their efforts as essential to the raising even of minimal consciousness about the inferior status of women *under* the law. When she turns her attention to the question of equal educational opportunity for women, Wallach argues that so lengthy a period of inequality justifies compensation. Thus she recommends preferential treatment to achieve parity of opportunity, and then concludes that if equal educational opportunity for women cannot be achieved in the presently male-dominated and male-biased law schools, that separate feminist institutions be established.

To look closely at any institution is to discover the power of men over the lives of women in and around that institution. Wallach's essay, like the others in this volume, is divided by an awareness of the formidable power of male-conceived and male-controlled law and by an intense desire to see feminism as powerful enough to overthrow that empire—not in exchange for an equally oppressive matriarchy, but rather to achieve the equalization of power in an egalitarian society that fosters self-determination and self-actualization for women as well as men, and without the exploitation of any group or class for the benefit of another. On the subject of feminist power, Rich will probably seem most optimistic—she is the most articulate about the current "feminist renaissance"—but she has been further away from the male centers of university and legal power than Hochschild, Wallach, or I.

I chose, for several reasons, to write about instrumental power, the tool of political leaders, administrators, teachers, and husbands. I chose to write about power because it is one subject that feminists have avoided for the past decade, and that earlier feminists have often scanted. It is also an essential subject, if the movement is to affect institutions as well as individual lives. But how to gain and use power without abusing others in the process? How to change institutions, and not merely the gender of the leadership at the top?

My essay grows out of several kinds of experiences. As a graduate student in the early fifties and as a college teacher in the decade before 1964, I was a grateful, passive woman who kept her "place" without knowing of its existence. The social and political movements of the sixties destroyed my passivity and led me to understand the power of leadership. I used my abilities as a teacher to organize people; I learned from organizing people how to teach more effectively. In each case, the long-range goal was similar: to share my consciousness and knowledge and thus to energize people, not to control them. Education thus conceived was not to be confused with power, but as a necessary precursor to it. Education was, in that sense, movement building.

After examining women's studies as one educational strategy for change, my essay concludes by asking a question: what strategies for change might a power-conscious base of academic women adopt during the next decade? In answering this question, I consider and debate the report of the Carnegie Commission on women. In sum, my view is that women should focus on building their potential for strong and effective leadership in those areas where they are currently numerically dominant—education, social work, nursing, for example—rather than diluting their possible power base by urging that those most energetic and talented serve as additional tokens in nontraditional fields of study.

The chapter on power concludes the book, but it is with that concept that the book was begun and that it was organized and written. The women who have written these essays share that vision of power, not simply as my collaborators, but as members of a broad-based women's movement. If many in that movement first eschewed power as "male," many more have since decided to reexamine its theory and practice. This book is one of those attempts.

1. Toward a Woman-Centered University

by Adrienne Rich

1

Early in my thinking about this essay, it had two titles. The first stands at the head of this page. The second grew out of a passage in Mary Beard's *Woman as Force in History,* where she describes the conditions of thought and education at the time of the Renaissance, prior to discussing the role played by women in intellectual life.

With the revival of classical learning came the humanizing of intellectual interest, knowledge, and public measures; that is, thought and action were directed by this learning to human concerns, as distinguished from the divine, and to the human race in general, as distinguished from individual salvation and particular peoples. . . .

In the promotion of the new learning, two tasks had to be carried out. The first included the recovery of additional classical works, the preparation of critical editions, the re-issue of the best . . . and critical study of the new texts. The second was the dissemination of the knowledge obtained from this critical study.

In the dissemination of the new learning . . . five methods were widely and intensively employed: tutoring and self-directed study in families, education in schools, humanist lecturing, conversations in small private groups and larger coteries, and correspondence (Beard, 1971, p. 260).

I had just been reading the syllabi of women's studies programs and courses all over the country, and it was natural to translate Beard's description into terms of this new curriculum, as well as of the feminist study groups, conferences, periodicals, and "conversations in small private groups and larger coteries" that have become legion over the past few years. And so for a while the working title of this essay was "Notes toward a

Feminist Renaissance." It is by now clear that a feminist renaissance is under way, that in the struggle to discover woman and her buried or misread history, feminists are doing two things: questioning and reexploring the past, and demanding a humanization of intellectual interests and public measures in the present. In the course of this work, lost sources of knowledge and of spiritual vitality are being recovered, while familiar texts are receiving a fresh critical appraisal, and the whole process is powered by a shift in perspective far more extraordinary and influential than the shift from theology to humanism of the European Renaissance. Much of this research, discussion, and analysis is already being carried on in the university, but even more is taking place outside it, in precisely the kind of unofficial, self-created groups described by Mary Beard. It could be said that a women's university-without-walls exists already in America, in the shape of women reading and writing with a new purposeful-ness, and the growth of feminist bookstores, presses, bib-liographic services, women's centers, medical clinics, libraries, art galleries, and workshops, all with a truly educational mission; and that the members of this university are working and studying out of intense concern for the quality of human life as distinct from the ego-bound achievement of individual success.[1] With the existence of the duplicating machine, documents, essays, poems, statistical tables are moving from hand to hand, passing through the mails; the "dissemination of the knowledge obtained from this study" is not accountable in terms of the sales

---

[1] "Throughout the United States women are forming their own law firms and legal clinics, establishing their own business companies, running their own printing presses, publishing their own magazines and newspapers, starting their own credit unions, banks, anti-rape squads, art galleries and schools, hospitals, non-sexist playgroups and child care centers, bands, theater groups, restaurants, literary magazines and scholarly journals. . . . These projects express a rejection of the values of existing institutional structures and, unlike the male hip counter-culture, represent an active attempt to reshape culture through changing values and consciousness. Feminist law firms press to change the laws regarding women's legal status; but they are equally concerned to change public awareness of women's second-class legal status. The self-help movement developed not only as an alternative to the authoritarian treatment women receive from male doctors, but also to change women's consciousness about their bodies. Feminist art schools and galleries exist not only to overcome discrimination against women in the art world, but also to sharpen women's consciousness about the nature and sources of their creativity. Self-help divorce coops strive not just for cheap divorces but to change attitudes about women's subordinate role in marriage" (Grimstad & Rennie, 1973, p. 7).

of a single edition or even dependent solely on commercial publication.

I returned to my original title—less elegant, more blunt, some might say more provocative—because immense forces in the university, as in the whole patriarchal society, are intrinsically opposed to anything resembling an actual feminist renaissance, wherever that process appears to be a serious undertaking and not merely a piece of decorative reformism. If the phrase "woman-centered university" sounds outrageous, biased, or improbable, we need only try the sound of its opposite, the "man-centered university"—not forgetting that grammar reveals the truth and that "man," the central figure of that earlier renaissance, was indeed the male, as he still is. Or, as the catalog of one "coeducational" institution has it:

Brandeis University has set itself to develop the whole man, the sensitive, cultured, open-minded citizen who grounds his thinking in facts, who is intellectually and spiritually aware, who believes that life is significant, and who is concerned with society and the role he will play in it (Brandeis University Bulletin, 1972–1973, p. 11).

This is no semantic game or trivial accident of language. What we have at present *is* a man-centered university, a breeding ground not of humanism, but of masculine privilege. As women have gradually and reluctantly been admitted into the mainstream of higher education, they have been made participants in a system that prepares men to take up roles of power in a man-centered society, that asks questions and teaches "facts" generated by a male intellectual tradition, and that both subtly and openly confirms men as the leaders and shapers of human destiny both within and outside academia. The exceptional women who have emerged from this system and who hold distinguished positions in it are just that: the required exceptions used by every system to justify and maintain itself. That all this is somehow "natural" and reasonable is still an unconscious assumption even of many who grant that women's role in society is changing, and that it needs to change.[2]

---

[2] According to the U.S. Office of Education's *Report on Higher Education* (Washington, D.C., 1971): "Our study found that discrimination against women, in contrast to that against minorities, is still overt and socially acceptable within the academic community." Quoted in K. Patricia Cross (1972, p. 49ff).

Since this condition reflects the unspoken—and outspoken—assumptions of man-centered society, it would be naive to imagine that the university per se can be a vanguard for change. It is probable that the unrecognized, unofficial university-without-walls I have described will prove a far more important agent in reshaping the foundations on which human life is now organized. The orthodox university is still a vital spot, however, if only because it is a place where people can find each other and begin to hear each other. (It is also a source of certain kinds of power. See Leffler, Gillespie, & Ratner, 1973, p. 7.) Women in the university therefore need to address themselves—against the opprobrium and obstruction they do and will encounter—to changing the center of gravity of the institution as far as possible; to work for a woman-centered university because only if that center of gravity can be shifted will women really be free to learn, to teach, to share strength, to explore, to criticize, and to convert knowledge to power. It will be objected that this is merely "reverse chauvinism." But given the intensive training all women go through in every society to place our own long-term and collective interests second or last and to value altruism at the expense of independence and wholeness—and given the degree to which the university reinforces that training in its every aspect—the most urgent need at present is for women to recognize, and act on, the priority of re-creating ourselves and each other, after our centuries of intellectual and spiritual blockading. A by-product of such a shift in priorities will of course ultimately mean an opening-out of intellectual challenges for men who are emotionally mature and intuitively daring enough to recognize the extent to which man-centered culture has also limited and blindered them.

A few male scholars have been examining the academic tradition from the point of view of its sexual bias. Walter J. Ong, S.J., suggests that the very origins of academic style are peculiarly masculine.

Rhetoric . . . developed in the past as a major expression of the rational level of the ceremonial combat which is found among males and typically only among males at the physical level throughout the entire animal kingdom. . . . Rhetoric became particularly attached to Learned Latin, which the male psyche appropriated to itself as an extrafamilial language when Latin ceased to be a "mother" tongue (that is, was no longer spoken in the home by one's mother). Latin, spoken and written for 1500 years with totally negligible exceptions only by males, became a ceremonial language institutionalizing with particular force the ceremonial polemic which set the style for all education until romanticism. For until the romantic age, academic education was all but exclusively focused on defending a position (thesis) or attacking the position of another person—even medicine was taught this way (Ong, 1972).

Ong remarks that "the ancient art of rhetoric did not and could not survive coeducation"—a statement that unfortunately is true only in the most literal sense.

A contemporary view is provided by Leonard Kriegel.

. . . my teachers at Columbia . . . knew the value of reputation, and they would bank it with all the fierce pride of Wall St. lawyers. . . . The process of attaining a reputation was part of a Columbia graduate education, and we were exposed to it as soon as classes began. A man needed reserve and style and distance here; intelligence was not enough. . . .

The "name" professors, those faculty whose shoulders were burdened with the reputation of the department, possessed that distance and propriety. They possessed other qualities, too. Some of them possessed contempt for their students. . . . Two professors of modern drama dueled each other for students, insisted on declarations of allegiance, of commitment not to a critical perspective but to themselves. . . .

I soon found out that importance was measured not in terms of scholarship but of power within the department. The majority of graduate students . . . were so caught up in the game, so victimized by their desire for careers, so willing to preserve a place at any cost at the side of some academic eminence, that their lives became mere extensions of the dehumanization of the university. . . . We emulated our models, working for the day when we, too, might claim professorial status for ourselves . . . worshippers at the shrine of making it.

. . . For most of us, the academic world had promised a way in which we could ignore the lure of materialism. Unfortunately, we turned into the consenting victims of what we claimed to ignore. If a student wished to buy the academic world, then it followed that he had to buy the rest of America also (Kriegel, 1972, pp. 43–44, 49–51).

Certain terms in the above quotations have a familiar ring: *defending, attacking, combat, status, banking, dueled, power, making it.* They suggest the connections—actual and metaphoric—between the style of the university and the style of a society invested in military and economic aggression. In each of these accounts what stands out is not the passion for "learning for its own sake" or the sense of an intellectual community, but the dominance of the masculine ideal, the race of men against one another, the conversion of an end to a means. If the university can thus become an alienating environment even for the men who have primary rights within it, it is an insidiously exploitative environment for women.

A number of other male writers have begun to acknowledge the sexual roots of the failure of masculine culture, and of the masculine order characterized by depersonalization, fragmentation, waste, artificial scarcity, and emotional shallowness, not to mention its suicidal obsession with power and technology as ends rather than as means. Some predict the reemergence of the "feminine principle" as the salvation of the species. For recent statements of this kind, one by a sociologist and one by a poet, see Philip Slater's *The Pursuit of Loneliness:* "Women are in a better position to liberate our society emotionally" (1970, p. 89) or Robert Bly's essay, "I Came Out of the Mother Naked": ". . . the Great Mother is moving again in the psyche. Every day her face becomes clearer" (1973, pp. 29–51). However, even when these writers acknowledge the problem as rooted in sexual disbalance, they seem to hope for some miraculous transformation of values brought about, not by actual women working to change actual conditions and exercising actual power, but by an intangible "feminine principle" or "mother consciousness." Neither Bly nor Slater acknowledges the existence of a women's movement or talks about how it might affect men; Slater in fact ignorantly and complacently predicted, as late as 1970, that "such is extremely unlikely to occur." Herbert Marcuse sees the women's liberation movement as a "radical force" and a "free society" as a "*female* society"; he hastens to add that this "has nothing to do with matriarchy of any sort," but with the "*femalization* of the male" (to be achieved through what specifics he does not tell us). He never deals with the fact that it is, after all, men who have created and profited from patriarchy, except insofar as he suggests that "the patriarchal society has created a female image, a female counter-force, which may still become one of the gravediggers of patriarchal society." (Somehow, the women's movement would seem to have been created by men.)

"In this sense too, the woman holds the promise of liberation" (Marcuse, 1972, pp. 75–78).

Evidently, it is not to men that we shall be looking for more concrete and less wishful thinking about centers of change, or new constructs by which change may become diffused through the society. This essay is an attempt to suggest some ways in which one particular institution—the university—might become a focus and magnet for a "female counter-force." My description will be tentative and partial; it would be premature and absurd to assume that we know precisely what forms will best accommodate the changes we want, or that the forms themselves will not change and develop. And, of course, my description presupposes simultaneous changes in every other cell of the social body.

2

The early feminists, the women intellectuals of the past, along with educated men, assumed that the intellectual structure as well as the contents of the education available to men was viable: that is, enduring, universal, a discipline civilizing to the mind and sensitizing to the spirit. Its claims for both humanism and objectivity went unquestioned. One of the few voices to question this was that of Virginia Woolf, in her still little-read and extraordinary *Three Guineas,* an essay connecting the causes of war and exploitation directly with the patriarchal system, and with the exclusion of women from learning and power. Far more radical in its vision than the more famous *A Room of One's Own,* it does not simply protest this exclusion but questions the very nature of the professions as practiced by men, the very quality of the intellectual heritage protected by the university.

The questions that we have to ask and to answer about that (academic) procession during this moment of transition are so important that they may well change the lives of all men and women forever. For we have to ask ourselves, here and now, do we wish to join that procession, or don't we? On what terms shall we join that procession? Above all, where is it leading us, the procession of educated men? . . . Let us never cease from thinking,—what is this "civilization" in which we find ourselves? What are these ceremonies and why should we take part in them? What are these professions and why should we make money out of them? Where in short is it leading us, the procession of the sons of educated men? (Woolf, 1938, 1966, pp. 62–63).

The major educational question for the nineteenth and earlier twentieth centuries was whether the given educational structure and contents should be made available to women. In the nineteenth century the issue to be resolved was whether a woman's mind and body were intended by "nature" to grapple with intellectual training.[3] In the first 60 years of our own century the "problem" seemed to be that education was "wasted" on women who married, had families, and effectively retired from intellectual life. These issues, of course, though they had to be argued, really veiled (as the question of "standards" veils the issue of nonwhite participation in higher education) the core of politics and social power. Why women gave up their careers after marriage, why even among the unmarried or childless so few were found in the front ranks of intellectual life were questions that opened up only when women began to ask them and explore the answers.

Until the 1960s, the university continued to be seen as a privileged enclave, somehow more defensible than other privileged enclaves, criticized if at all for being too idealistic, too little in touch with the uses and abuses of power; and romanticized as a place where knowledge is loved for its own sake, every opinion has an open-minded hearing, "the dwelling place of permanent values . . . of beauty, of righteousness, of freedom," as the Brandeis University bulletin intones. The radical student critique—black and white—of the sixties readily put its finger on the facts underlying this fiction: the racism of the academy and its curriculum, its responsiveness to pressures of vested interest, political, economic and military; the use of the academy as a base for research into weapons and social control and as a machinery for perpetuating the power of white, middle-class men. Today the question is no longer whether women (or nonwhites) are intellectually and "by nature" equipped for higher education, but whether this male-created, male-dominated structure is really capable of serving the humanism and freedom it professes.

---

[3] "To intellectuals like Henry Adams and G. Stanley Hall, the learned woman threatened not only the American home but the very survival of the race. Turning an energy properly altruistic and collective into individual self-consciousness, deflecting blood to the brain from the 'generative organs,' with atrophied mammary glands and irregular periodicity, she had lost touch with the sacred primitive rhythms that bound her to the 'deepest law of the cosmos'" (B. Cross, 1965, pp. 37–38).

Woolf suggested that women entering the professions must bring with them the education—unofficial, unpaid for, unvalued by society—of their female experience, if they are not to become subject to the dehumanizing forces of competition, money lust, the lure of personal fame and individual aggrandizement, and "unreal loyalties." In other words, we must choose what we will accept and what we will reject of institutions already structured and defined by patriarchal values. Today, more crucial even than the number of teaching jobs open to women—crucial as that continues to be—is the process of deciding "on what terms we shall join that procession." Woolf, for all the charges of lack of class consciousness thrown at her, was in fact extremely conscious of the evils of exclusivity and elitism. She had to a marked degree the female knowledge of what it means to be kept outside, alienated from power and knowledge, and of how subtly a place "inside" corrupts even liberal spirits.

> . . . the professions have a certain undeniable effect upon the professors. They make the people who practise them possessive, jealous of any infringement of their rights, and highly combative if anyone dares dispute them. . . . Therefore this guinea, which is to help you help women to enter the professions, has this condition as a first condition attached to it. You shall swear that you will do all in your power to insist that any woman who enters any profession shall in no way hinder any other human being, whether man or woman, white or black, provided that he or she is qualified to enter that profession, from entering it; but shall do all in her power to help them (Woolf, 1938, 1966, p. 66).

What Woolf could not then have recognized, what the present-day radical feminist has come to recognize, is that in order to become a force against elitism and exclusivity we must learn to place each other and ourselves first, not to hinder other human beings, but to tap the kinds of power and knowledge that exist—buried, diffused, misnamed, sometimes misdirected—within women.[4] At this point we need the university, with its

---

[4] The urge to leap across feminism to "human liberation" is a tragic and dangerous mistake. It deflects us from our real sources of vision, recycles us back into old definitions and structures, and continues to serve the purposes of patriarchy, which will use "women's lib," as it contemptuously phrases it, only to buy more time for itself—as both capitalism and socialism are now doing. Feminism is a criticism and subversion of *all* patriarchal thought and institutions—not merely those currently seen as reactionary and tyrannical.

libraries, laboratories, archives, collections, and some—but not all—of the kinds of trained thinking and expertise it has to offer. We need to consciously and critically select what is genuinely viable and what we can use from the masculine intellectual tradition, as we possess ourselves of the knowledge, skills, and perspectives that can refine our goal of self-determination with discipline and wisdom. (Certainly we do *not* need the university to continue replicating the tradition that has excluded us, or to become "amateur males.") The university is not the only place where this work will be carried on; nor, obviously, can the university become more woman-centered and less elitist while the society remains androcentric.

3

There are two ways in which a woman's integrity is likely to be undermined by the process of university education. This education is, of course, yet another stage in the process of her entire education, from her earliest glimpses of television at home to the tracking and acculturating toward "femininity" that become emphatic in high school. But when a woman is admitted to higher education—particularly graduate school—it is often made to sound as if she enters a sexually neutral world of "disinterested" and "universal" perspectives. It is assumed that coeducation means the equal education, side by side, of women and men. Nothing could be further from the truth; and nothing could more effectively seal a woman's sense of her secondary value in a man-centered world than her experience as a "privileged" woman in the university—if she knows how to interpret what she lives daily.

In terms of the *content* of her education, there is no discipline that does not obscure or devalue the history and experience of women as a group. What Otto Rank said of psychology has to be said of every other discipline, including the "neutral" sciences: it is "not only man-made . . . but masculine in its mentality" (Rank, 1941, p. 37). Will it seem, in 40 years, astonishing that a book should have been written in 1946 with the title *Woman as Force in History?* The title does not seem bizarre to us now. Outside of women's studies, though liberal male professors may introduce material about women into their courses, we live with textbooks, research studies, scholarly sources, and lectures that treat women as a subspecies, mentioned only as peripheral to the history of men. In every discipline where we *are* considered, women are perceived as the objects rather than the originators of inquiry, thus primarily through male eyes, thus as a special category. That the true business of civilization has been in the hands of men is the lesson absorbed by every student of the traditional sources. How this came to be, and the process that kept it so, may well be the most important question for the self-understanding and survival of the human species; but the extent to which civilization has been built on the bodies and services of women—unacknowledged, unpaid, and unprotested in the main—is a subject apparently unfit for scholarly decency. The witch persecutions of the fourteenth through seventeenth centuries, for example, involved one of the great historic struggles—a class struggle and a struggle for knowledge—between the illiterate but practiced female healer and the beginnings of an aristocratic nouveau science, between the powerful patriarchal Church and enormous numbers of peasant women, between the pragmatic experience of the wisewoman and the superstitious practices of the early male medicine (Ehrenreich & English, 1973). The phenomena of woman-fear and woman-hatred illuminated by these centuries of gynocide are with us still; certainly a history of psychology or history of science that was not hopelessly one-sided would have to confront and examine this period and its consequences. Like the history of slave revolts, the history of women's resistance to domination awaits discovery by the offspring of the dominated. The chronicles, systems, and investigations of the humanities and the sciences are in fact a collection of half-truths and lacunae that have worked enormous damage to the ability of the sexes to understand themselves and one another.

If this is changing within the rubric of women's studies, it is doing so in the face of prejudice, contempt, and outright obstruction. If it is true that the culture recognized and transmitted by the university has been predominantly white Western culture, it is also true that within black and Third World studies the emphasis is still predominantly masculine, and the female perspective needs to be fought for and defended there as in the academy at large.

I have been talking about the content of the university curriculum, that is, the mainstream of the curriculum. Women in colleges where a women's studies program already exists, or where feminist courses are beginning to be taught, still are often made to feel that the "real" curriculum is the male-centered one; that women's studies are (like Third World studies) a "fad"; that feminist teachers are "unscholarly," "unprofessional," or "dykes." But the content of courses and programs is only the more concrete form of undermining experienced by the woman student. More invisible, less amenable to change by committee proposal or fiat, is the hierarchal image, the structure of relationships, even the style of discourse, including assumptions about theory and practice, ends and means, process and goal.

The university is above all a hierarchy. At the top is a small cluster of highly paid and prestigious persons, chiefly men, whose careers entail the services of a very large base of ill-paid or unpaid persons, chiefly women: wives, research assistants, secretaries, teaching assistants, cleaning women, waitresses in the faculty club, lower-echelon administrators, and women students who can be used in various ways to gratify the ego. Each of these groups of women sees itself as distinct from the others, as having different interests and a different destiny. The student may become a research assistant, mistress, or even wife; the wife may act as secretary or personal typist for her husband, or take a job as lecturer or minor administrator; the graduate student may, if she demonstrates unusual brilliance and carefully follows the rules, rise higher into the pyramid, where she loses her identification with teaching fellows, as the wife forgets her identification with the student or secretary she may once have been. The waitress or cleaning woman has no such mobility, and it is rare for other women in the university, beyond a few socially aware or feminist students, to support her if she is on strike or unjustly fired. Each woman in the university is defined by her relationship to the men in power instead of her relationship to other women up and down the scale.

Now, this fragmentation among women is merely a replication of the fragmentation from each other that women undergo in the society outside; in accepting the premise that advancement and security—even the chance to do one's best work—lie in propitiating and identifying with men who have some power, we have always found ourselves in competition with each other and blinded to our common struggles. This fragmentation and the invisible demoralization it generates work constantly against the intellectual and emotional energies of the woman student.

The hidden assumptions on which the university is built comprise more than simply a class system. In a curious and insidious way the "work" of a few men—especially in the more scholarly and prestigious institutions—becomes a sacred value in whose name emotional and economic exploitation of women is taken for granted. The distinguished professor may understandably like comfort and even luxury and his ego requires not merely a wife and secretary but an *au pair* girl, teaching assistant, programmer, and student mistress; but the justification for all this service is the almost religious concept of "his work." (Those few women who rise to the top of their professions seem in general to get along with less, to get their work done along with the cooking, personal laundry, and mending without the support of a retinue.) In other words, the structure of the man-centered university constantly reaffirms *the use of women as means* to the end of male "work"—meaning male careers and professional success. Professors of Kantian ethics or Marxist criticism are no more exempt from this exploitation of women than are professors of military science or behavioral psychology. In its very structure, then, the university encourages women to continue perceiving themselves as means and not as ends—as indeed their whole socialization has done.

It is sometimes pointed out that because the majority of women working in the university are in lower-status positions, the woman student has few if any "role models" she can identify with in the form of women professors or even high-ranking administrators. She therefore can conceive of her own future only in terms of limited ambitions. But it should be one of the goals of a woman-centered university to do away with the pyramid itself, insofar as it is based on sex, age, color, class, and other irrelevant distinctions. I will take this up again further on.

4

For reasons both complex and painful, the "exceptional" woman who receives status and tenure in the university has often been less than supportive to young women beginning their own careers. She has for her own survival learned to vote against other women, absorb the masculine adversary style of discourse, and carefully avoid any style or method that could be condemned as "irrational" or "emotionally charged." She chooses for investigation subjects as remote as possible from her self-interest as a woman,[5] or if women are the objects of her investigation, she manages to write about them as if they belonged to a distant tribe. The kinds of personal knowledge and reflection that might illuminate the study of, say, death fantasies during pregnancy, or the recurrent figure of the Beautiful Dead Woman in male art, or that might lead to research on a method of birth control comparable with other developments in medicine and technology—such are ruled out lest she appear "unscholarly" or "subjective." (It is a grotesque fact that the literature available on the female orgasm and on lesbianism is almost entirely by male researchers.) Of course, the advent of feminist studies has been rapidly changing this scene, and will continue to change it. But again, the usually younger feminist scholar-teacher is in most places untenured and struggling, and the style and concerns of masculine scholarship still represent the mainstream.

The mental hospital and the psychotherapeutic situation have been described as replicating the situation of women in the patriarchal family (Chesler, 1972, p. 35). The university is likewise a replica of the patriarchal family. The male teacher may have a genuinely "fatherly" relation to his gifted student-daughter, and many intellectual women have been encouraged and trained by their gifted fathers, or gifted male teachers. But it is the *absence* of the brilliant and creative mother, or woman teacher, that is finally of more importance than the presence of the brilliant and creative male. Like the favorite daughter in the patriarchal family, the promising woman student comes to identify with her male scholar-teacher more strongly than with her sisters. He may well be in a position to give her more, in terms of influence, training, and emotional gratification, than any academic woman on the scene. In a double sense, he confirms her suspicion that she is "exceptional." If she succeeds, it is partly that she has succeeded in pleasing *him,* winning his masculine interest and attention. The eroticism of the father-daughter relationship resonates here, and romance and flirtation

---

[5] "Until recently, most academic women have avoided women's subjects like the plague; to do otherwise was to diminish their chances of being considered serious contenders in traditionally male fields" (Sicherman, 1972, p. 76). Leffler et al. (1974, pp. 12–13) suggest that although more recently a reverse trend is seen among "academic feminists," they "rarely research new topics or develop new ideas on the gender problem. Rather, they tend to trail in the movement's wake . . . (without acknowledging movement inspiration, naturally)."

are invisibly present even where there is no actual seduction. Alice Rossi has pointed out the potential undermining of a woman's self-confidence when she is engaged in an actual sexual alliance with her mentor: how can she be sure that his praise is not a form of seduction, that her recommendations were not won in bed? (Rossi, 1973, Ch. 21). And not infrequently the professor marries his gifted woman student and secures her for life as a brain as well as a body, the critic and editor of his books, "without whom . . . ," as the dedications all say. A woman-centered university would be a place in which the much-distorted mother-daughter relationship could find a new model: where women of maturer attainments in every field would provide intellectual guidance along with concern for the wholeness of their young women students, an older woman's sympathy and unique knowledge of the processes younger women were going through, along with the power to give concrete assistance and support. Under such circumstances it is likely that far less eroticism would glamorize the male teacher, and the woman student could use whatever he had to offer her without needing to identify with him or adopt his perspective for her own.[6]

5

I have tried to show that the androcentric university not only undermines and exploits women but forces men who wish to succeed in it further into the cul-de-sac of one-sided masculinity. In this it is simply a microcosm of society. Virginia Woolf was a forerunner of contemporary feminist analysts in criticizing the drive for goals without consideration of means and process, the glorification of competition, the confusion between human beings and objects as products of this one-sided masculinity of culture; and in this century we have seen culture brought low and discredited because of them. Without pretending that we can in our present stage of understanding and of mystification through language define crisply and forever what is "masculine" and what is "feminine," we *can* at least say that the above corruptions and confusions are products of a male-dominated history.

---

[6] For the other side of the coin—exclusion of women from the protégé system on a sexual basis—see The American Sociological Association (1973, pp. 26–28). On both sides of the coin, dependency on the male teacher is the rule.

The world as a whole is rapidly becoming Westernized. In no culture more than in Western culture is the failure of ideas like "industrialization" and "development" more evident; for without famine, without authentic scarcity, without the naked struggle to stay alive, and with the apparent "freedom" of unveiled and literate women, the condition of woman has remained that of a nonadult, a person whose exploitation—physical, economic, or psychic—is accepted *no matter to what class she belongs.* A society that treats any group of adults as nonadult—that is, unfit to assume utmost responsibility in society and unfit for doing the work of their choice—will end by treating most of its citizens as patriarchal society has treated children—that is, lying to them and using force, overt or manipulative, to control them.

I want to suggest two categories of women's needs that would, if genuinely met, change the nature of the university and to some extent the community outside the university, and I am suggesting further that these needs of women are congruent with the humanizing of the community-at-large. The first category includes both the content of education and the style in which it is treated. The second includes institutionalized obstacles that effectively screen out large numbers of able women from full or partial engagement in higher education.

First, as to curriculum: As the hitherto "invisible" and marginal agent in culture, whose native culture has been effectively denied, women need a reorganization of knowledge, of perspectives and analytical tools that can help us know our foremothers, evaluate our present historical, political, and personal situation, and take ourselves seriously as agents in the creation of a more balanced culture. Some feminists foresee this culture as based on female primacy, others as "androgynous"; whatever it is to become, women will have the primary hand in its shaping. This does not and need not mean that the entire apparatus of masculine intellectual achievement should be scrapped, or that women should simply turn the whole apparatus inside out and substitute "she" for "he." Some of the structures will be seen as unhealthy for human occupation even while their grandeur in its own day can be appreciated; like an old and condemned building, we may want to photograph these for posterity and tear them down; some may be reconstructed along different lines; some we may continue to live in and use. But a radical reinvention of subject, lines of inquiry, and method will be required. As Mary Daly has written:

The tyranny of methodolatry hinders new discoveries. It prevents us from raising questions never asked before and from being illumined by ideas that do not fit into pre-established boxes and forms. . . . Under patriarchy, Method has wiped out women's questions so totally that even women have not been able to hear and formulate our own questions to meet our own experiences (Daly, 1973, pp. 11–12).

Daly also calls for "breaking down the barriers between technical knowledge and that deep realm of intuitive knowledge which some theologians call ontological reason" (ibid., p. 39). In fact, it is in the realm of the apparently unimpeachable sciences that the greatest modifications and revaluations will undoubtedly occur. It may well be in this domain that has proved least hospitable or attractive to women—theoretical science—that the impact of feminism and of woman-centered culture will have the most revolutionary impact. It was a woman, Simone Weil, who wrote, in the early thirties:

. . . the technicians are ignorant of the theoretical basis of the knowledge which they employ. The scientists in their turn not only remain out of touch with technical problems but in addition are cut off from that over-all vision which is the very essence of theoretical culture. One could count on one's fingers the number of scientists in the entire world who have a general idea of the history and development of their own particular science; there is not one who is really competent as regards sciences other than his own . . . (Rees, 1966, pp. 20–21).

A more recent writer points out the historical origins for the scientist's claim to neutrality, his (*sic*) assertion of normative freedom, and his "conscious rejection and ignorance of the subjective and the a-rational in human activity" (Mendelsohn, 1973, p. 48). He suggests that every attempt to bring public and social sanctions to bear on the scientist's designs has hitherto met with defeat and that every attempt to extend the boundaries of accepted epistemology, including psychoanalysis, has been labeled "pseudoscience." (He fails, however, to mention the healing and midwifery of wisewomen that were even more violently driven underground. Mendelsohn's article, in fact, though it is concerned with the return of science to the service of human needs, and though it was delivered as a lecture to a Radcliffe Institute symposium on women, never touches on the connection between the masculinization of the sciences and their elitism, indifference to values, and rigidity of method.) He ends, however, by calling for certain kinds of change in the procedures and priorities of the science that can be applied by extension to the entire body of knowledge and method that the university has adopted for its province:

A reconstructed science would value truth, but also compassion. It would have an inbuilt ethic that would defend both being and living; that is, knowledge that would be non-violent, non-coercive, non-exploitative, non-manipulative . . . that would renounce finally the Faustian quest to achieve the limits of the universe or total knowledge, that would work to construct models that would be more explanatory and more inclusive—science practiced among and derived from the public. What if we were to say that we would not undertake to develop what could not be understood and publicly absorbed, that we were intent on building a science not confined to academies and institutions (ibid., p. 52).

Certainly a major change will be along the lines already seen in women's studies: a breakdown of traditional departments and "disciplines," of that fragmentation of knowledge that weakens thought and permits the secure ignorance of the specialist to protect him from responsibility for the applications of his theories. It is difficult to imagine a woman-centered curriculum where quantitative method and technical reason would continue to be allowed to become means for the reduction of human lives, and where specialization would continue to be used as an escape from wholeness.[7]

It has been almost a given of women's courses that style and content are inseparable. A style has evolved in the classroom, more dialogic, more exploratory, less given to pseudo-

---

[7] Mina P. Shaughnessy has written of the failures of measurement to account for actual events in the teaching process: "In how many countless and unconscious ways do we capitulate to the demand for numbers? . . . In how many ways has the need for numbers forced us to violate the language itself, ripping it from the web of discourse in order to count those things that can be caught in the net of numbers?" (Shaughnessy, 1973).

objectivity, than the traditional mode. A couple of examples of the feminist approach are quoted below. The first comes from a description of an applied psychology course on discrimination against women, taught at the University of Wales in Cardiff:

A "personal style" was adopted. By this I mean a style of communication which avoided such constructions as "it is said," "it is thought," "it is considered." In short, I acknowledged the subjective element by not avoiding the use of the personal pronoun. This style is more appropriate to a non-exploitative, non-patriarchal interaction between students and teacher. It is conducive to a greater degree of academic rigour. . . . It seems to me that the form of many communications in academia, both written and verbal, is such as to not only obscure the influence of the personal or subjective but also to give the impression of divine origin—a mystification composed of sybilline statements—from beings supposedly emptied of the "dross" of self. Additionally I believe that a "personal style" probably encourages greater creativeness. Further, it seems to me, that, when teaching, such a style encourages the active involvement of all concerned. It is opposed to any form of alienation. It seems particularly appropriate that women's studies should counteract the misleading tendency in academe to camouflage the influence of the subject (Rosenfelt, 1973, p. 10).

The second example comes from the actual syllabus handed to students in a course, "The Education of Women in Historical Perspective."

I am teaching this course because I believe that education is the key to social change. Despite the generally conservative role that formal institutions play in society, philosophers, statesmen and parents have looked to schools for improving the *status quo.* Access to schools has been used as a method of social control, as have curriculum and teaching methods. The schools can become vehicles for indoctrination, for oppression, as well as for healthy stimulation of individual and societal freedom; the line between "education" and indoctrination is difficult to define, but essential to look for.

. . . I look at issues historically; that has been my training, and my primary interest. I have trouble with the twentieth century, far preferring the puzzle of the nineteenth. In women's education, this was when the biggest changes took place, when education for women was a revolutionary question. However, we may be in the midst of another revolutionary time, and an understanding of the past is essential for appreciation of the contemporary scene. History can be a delightful escape into a world where there is a finite number of questions. . . . This course is my attempt to escape from my ostrich tendencies, to understand my own role in the present movement.

I want to stress this problem of bias because scholarship is supposed to be as bias-free as possible. We will look at all questions and issues from as many sides as we can think of; but I am inescapably a feminist. . . . You must question my assumptions, my sources, my information; that is part of learning to learn. You should also question your own assumptions. Skepticism about oneself is essential to continued growth and a balanced perspective (ibid., p. 187).

The underlying mode of the feminist teaching style is thus by nature antihierarchical.

6

I have described the university as a hierarchy built on exploitation. To become truly educated and self-aware, against the current of patriarchal education, a woman must be able to discover and explore her root connection with *all women.* Her previous education has taught her only of her prescribed relationships with men, or "Women beware women." Any genuine attempt to fill this need would become a force for the dehierarchizing of the university. For it would have to involve all women in the institution, simultaneously, as students and as teachers, besides drawing on the special experience of non-academic women, both within and outside the university—the grandmothers, the high school dropouts, the professionals, the artists, the political women, the housewives. And it would involve them at an organic level, not as interesting exhibits or specimens.

There is one crucial hub around which all the above revolves —one need that is primary if women are to assume any real equality in the academic world, one challenge that the university today, like the society around it, evades with every trick in its possession. This is the issue of child care. The welfare mother badgered to get out and work, the cafeteria worker whose child wears a latchkey, the student or assistant professor constantly uncertain about the source and quality of the next baby-sitter, all have this at stake; all are constantly forced to improvise or to give up in the struggle to fill this social vacuum. Full-time mothering is a peculiar and late-arrived social phenomenon (Slater, 1968, p.

450) and is assumed to be the "normal" mode of child rearing in the United States; but full-time mothering, even by choice, is not an option for the majority of women. There is no improvisation of child care—even if it be the child's own father who "generously" agrees to share the chores—that can begin to substitute for an excellent, dependable, nonsexist, imaginative system of care, cheap enough for all, and extending identical opportunities to the children of the poorest and the highest-paid women on the campus.

Alice Rossi has described some of the possibilities and practical solutions to this question in her "Equality between the Sexes: An Immodest Proposal" (in Lifton, 1968, pp. 121–124), and much of what I am going to say here will merely develop what she earlier sketched out. Perhaps I shall say it with a greater sense of urgency, because even in the years since her essay was written, the struggle over child care and the need for it have become more clear-cut. Attention to how children are to be cared for and socialized can be seen as a kind of test of the "humanism" of the university, which has hitherto been so responsive to the masters of war. In the past the university has *used* children, in its special kindergartens and laboratory schools, as guinea pigs for tests and new methods, just as it has used the community around it for such purposes.

The degree to which patriarchal society has neglected the problem of child care is in some ways reflective of its need to restrict the lives of women. Even in "revolutionary" socialist societies, where women are a needed sector of the labor force, and where state-supported collective child care exists, the centers are staffed by women and women bear the ultimate responsibility for children. This may not in itself be undesirable; but the relegation of this responsibility to women reflects a reactionary thinking about sexual roles rather than a conscious decision made in the light of a feminist analysis. In both China and the Soviet Union the grandmother is an important adjunct to collective day care; the grandfather goes unmentioned in this role.[8] In

---

[8] Ruth Sidel (1972, p. 25) reports of China: "All nursery and kindergarten teachers are women. There seems to be no effort to recruit men into fields in which they would be working with small children. And there seems to be no concern for breaking down the traditional sex roles in professions such as teaching and nursing, both of which are virtually all female." See also Toni Blanken, "Preschool Collectives in the Soviet Union," in Roby (1973, pp. 386–397).

the United States, the rapid increase in single-parent families and female heads of households does not alter the fact that, as of today, the fantasy of the family as consisting of a breadwinning father, a homemaking mother, and children is the model on which most social constructs are based. School holidays and lunch and coming-home hours, for example, often reflect the assumption that there is a nonworking mother whose major responsibility is to be there when the children come home. Even within the women's movement, child care for women who wish to be politically or culturally active is sometimes a neglected priority in the arranging of conferences and workshops.

It is difficult to imagine, unless one has lived it, the personal division, endless improvising, and creative and intellectual holding back that for most women accompany the attempt to combine the emotional and physical demands of parenthood and the challenges of work. To assume one can naturally combine these has been a male privilege everywhere in the world. For women, the energy expended in both the conflict and the improvisation has held many back from starting a professional career and has been a heavy liability to careers once begun. The few exceptions in this country have been personal solutions; for the majority of mothers no such options exist.

Since this essay is concerned, not with an ideal future but with some paths toward it, I am assuming that within the foreseeable future few if any adequate community children's centers will be available, certainly on the scale and of the excellence we need. Until such exist in every community, it will be necessary for any university concerned with shifting its androcentric imbalance to provide them. But again, they cannot be merely token custodial units, or testing grounds run by the university for its own experimental ends. The kind of child care I am going to describe would be designed first of all in the interests of the children and mothers it serves.

1 Child care would be available for children of all students, staff, and faculty, with additional places for community children, at a subsidized rate that would make it effectively open to all. This is an absolutely necessary, though not sufficient, condition for the kinds of change we envision.

2 Child care would be of the highest quality; no merely custodial center would be tolerated. The early nurture and education of the children

would be as flexible and imaginative as possible. There would be a conscious counterthrust against the sex-role programming of patriarchal society.

3   The centers would be staffed, under experienced and qualified directorship, by women and men who have chosen and been trained for this kind of work. They would be assisted by several kinds of people:

(a) College students, female and male, who want experience in early education or just want to spend time with children. (Several experienced baby-sitters could work with several times the number of children they ordinarily "sit" with in private homes, and with more expert supervision.)

(b) High school students similar to the college students in (a).

(c) Older women and men from the community—"grandparents" with special qualifications, informal or formal.

(d) Parents who want to share their children's lives on a part-time basis during the working day.

(e) Apprentices from graduate programs in education, pediatrics, psychology, the arts, etc.

The children would thus be in contact with a wide range of women and men, of different ages, as "nurturant" figures from an early age. The core staff of the centers should be as sexually balanced and as permanent as possible.

I am aware that some feminists, including some lesbian mothers, might prefer to see the nurture and acculturation of young children entirely in the hands of women—not as an acting out of traditional roles, but as a cultural and political choice. I tend, however, to agree with Michelle Rosaldo when she writes:

> . . . American society is . . . organized in a way that creates and exploits a radical distance between private and public, domestic and social, female and male . . . this conflict is at the core of the contemporary rethinking of sex roles. . . . If the public world is to open its doors to more than an elite among women, the nature of work itself will have to be altered, and the asymmetry between work and the home reduced. For this we must . . . bring men into the sphere of domestic concerns and responsibilities (Rosaldo & Lamphere, 1974, p. 42).

4   There should be flexibility enough to allow parents to, say, take their children to the university museum or for lunch in the cafeteria if they so desire. Nursing mothers should be able to come and feed their babies.

5 A well-baby clinic, with both medical and dental care, should be regularly provided for all the children as a service of the centers. A referral service for mothers with physical or psychic problems should be available.

6 There should be opportunities for staff and parents of the centers to discuss, in small groups, ideas of child rearing, criticisms of the running of the center, and ways in which it can better serve its clients.

While excellent universal early childhood care should be a major priority in any reasonably humane society, the primary and moving impulse behind the children's center would be to help equalize the position of women.[9]

7

The notion of the "full-time" student has penalized both women and the poor. The student with a full-time job and a full-time academic program is obviously more handicapped than the student who can afford to go to college without working. Many women—married, divorced, or single mothers—have the equivalent of an unpaid full-time job at home and are discouraged from considering advanced study. Until universal and excellent child care is developed these women are handicapped in undertaking a full-time program. Sometimes only a year or so of part-time study would make the difference between continuing their education and dropping out, or between real achievement and a frantic attempt to muddle through.[10]

[9] See Simmons and Chayes, "University Day Care," and Hagen, "Child Care and Women's Liberation," in Roby (1973). Obviously, day care is both an educational and a political issue and can evoke different ideas of goal and quality from different groups. For example, the heterosexual mother and the lesbian mother may each see quite different objectives for the kind of center in which she would want to place her child. (See *Ain't I A Woman*, double issue on child care, Spring 1973.) These differences will undoubtedly emerge and have to be worked through, sometimes painfully; but I agree with Gross and MacEwen (Roby, 1973, p. 295) that it must be the parents (I would say particularly the mothers) who establish goals for the center and that the university should be seen purely as a provider of space and funding.

[10] K. Patricia Cross (1972, p. 49ff) observes furthermore that "mature women constitute a significant segment of the [new student] population" and asserts the need for a recognition of American mobility (in which the wife is uprooted by the husband's career) through systems of transferable credits and credit-by-examination.

But in a university not dedicated primarily to reduplicating the old pyramid, two other groups will need the availability of part-time study. Women faculty should make it one of their special concerns that staff and community women be brought into the educational process. All staff—women and men—should have paid time off for auditing or taking courses for credit, as well as access to libraries and to academic counseling. Community women must be taken seriously as potential users of the university. Many of these women have suffered from the burdens of both race and sex; tracked into the nonacademic stream in high school, carrying the responsibilities of early marriages and large families, they have worked hard both within and outside the home and yet have often been dismissed in the most offhand stereotyping both by the radical male left and by male "liberals."

Whether invisible as scrubwomen or cafeteria workers, or vaguely perceived as shoppers in the local supermarket or mothers pushing prams in the community, these women are also becoming increasingly awake to expectations they have been denied.[11] The working women employed by the university and the women of its local community both have claims upon the resources it so jealously guards. They should be able to look to a nonelitist university for several kinds of resources: a women's health center, with birth control and abortion counseling, Pap tests, pamphlets, and talks on women's health problems; a rape crisis center; an adult education program in which women at first too shy or uncertain to enroll for college classes might test their interests and abilities (this might include remedial reading and writing, math, women's history, basic economics, current events, community organizing workshops, poetry and art workshops, etc.); a woman-staffed women's psychological counseling center with both group and individual counseling; a law clinic. A

---

[11] A recent *New York Times Magazine* article carried a series of transcribed conversations with middle-aged, mostly blue-collar, second-generation Italian and Jewish women in East Flatbush, all in their forties and members of a consciousness-raising group, all concerned with changing and expanding their lives now that their children are grown up. One recalls "how hard I fought for my girls to go to college." The author comments that "two main concerns spurred their interest in feminism: the feeling that society in general, and their husbands in particular, no longer viewed them as sexually interesting . . . and the realization that they were 'out of a job' in the same sense as a middle-aged man who is fired by his employer of 20 years" (Jacoby, 1973).

large university should be prepared to integrate services contributed to such centers with the other academic commitments of
any faculty member willing and qualified to work in them. And,
undoubtedly, a great deal of reciprocal education would be going
on as women of very different backgrounds and shades of
opinion began to meet, hold discussions, and discover their
common ground.

I can anticipate one response to these recommendations,
partly because it has been leveled at me in conversation, partly
because I have leveled it at myself. The university cannot, it may
be argued, become all to each; it cannot serve the education of
young adults, train future specialists, provide a conduit for
research and scholarship, and do all these other things you are
suggesting. I have, I confess, thought long and hard on that side
of the question. Part of my final resolution comes from the fact
that we are talking about a process involving simultaneous
changes both in society "out there" and in the university, and
that when the local or national community becomes able to
develop strong and responsive centers such as I have been
describing for all its citizens, the burden would not have to fall on
the university. Ideally, I imagine a very indistinct line between
"university" and "community" instead of the familiar city-on-a-
hill frowning down on its neighbors, or the wrought-iron gates
by which town and gown have traditionally understood their
relationship. For centuries women were by definition people of
the town, not of the gown; and still, there are many more of us
"down there."

Moreover, the university in contemporary America has not
been at such pains to refrain from providing services to *certain*
communities: consulting for industry and government, conduct-
ing classified military research, acting as a recruitment center for
the military-industrial and intelligence communities. What I am
really suggesting is that it change its focus but still continue its
involvement outside the ivy—or graffiti—covered walls. Instead
of serving such distant and faceless masters as the "challenge of
Sputnik," cold war "channeling," or the Air Force, a university
responsive to women's needs would serve the needs of the
human, visible community in which it sits—the neighborhood,
the city, the rural county, its true environment. In a sense the
solution I am proposing is anarchistic: that the university should
address itself to the microcosms of national problems and issues

that exist locally, and that it should do so with the greatest possible sense that it will not simply be giving, but be receiving, because academe has a great deal to learn from women and from other unprivileged people.

I have described the kinds of ad hoc teaching that might take place under university auspices. As a research institution, it should organize its resources around problems specific to its community; for example, adult literacy; public health; safer, cheaper, and simpler birth control; drug addiction; community action; geriatrics and the sociology and psychology of aging and death; the history and problems of women and those of people in nonwhite, non–middle-class cultures; urban (or rural) adolescence; public architecture; child development and pediatrics; urban engineering with the advice and consent of the engineered; folk medicine; the psychology, architecture, economics, and diet of prisons; union history; the economics of the small farmer—the possibilities would vary from place to place. The "community" is probably a misleading term. In fact, most large urban universities have many communities. The "community" around Columbia University, for example, is not simply black and Puerto Rican, but white middle-class, poor and aged, Jewish, Japanese, Cuban, etc. A sympathetic and concerned relationship with all these groups would involve members of the university in an extremely rich cluster of problems. And the nature of much research (and its usefulness) might be improved if it were conceived as research *for,* rather than *on,* human beings.

8

I have been trying to think of a celebrated literary utopia written by a woman. The few contenders would be contemporary: Monique Wittig's *Les Guerillères*—but that is really a vision of epic struggle, or Elizabeth Gould Davis's early chapters in *The First Sex*—but those are largely based on Bachofen. Shulamith Firestone noted the absence of a female utopia in *The Dialectic of Sex* and proceeded, in the last chapter, to invent her own. These thoughts occur because any vision of things-other-than-as-they-are tends to meet with the charge of "utopianism," so much power has the way-things-are to denude and impoverish the imagination. Even minds practiced in criticism of the status quo resist a vision so apparently unnerving as that which foresees an end to male privilege and a changed relationship between the sexes. The university I have been trying to imagine does not seem to me utopian, though the problems and contradictions to be faced in its actual transformation are of course real and severe. For a long time, academic feminists, like all feminists, are going to have to take personal risks—of confronting their own realities, of speaking their minds, of being fired or ignored when they do so, of becoming stereotyped as "man-haters" when they evince a primary loyalty to women. They will also encounter opposition from successful women who have been the token "exceptions." This opposition—this female misogyny—is a leftover of a very ancient competitiveness and self-hatred forced on women by patriarchal culture. What is now required of the fortunate exceptional women are the modesty and courage to see why and how they have been fortunate at the expense of other women, and to begin to acknowledge their community with them. As one of them has written:

The first responsibility of a "liberated" woman is to lead the fullest, freest and most imaginative life she can. The second responsibility is her solidarity with other women. She may live and work and make love with men. But she has no right to represent her situation as simpler, or less suspect, or less full of compromises than it really is. Her good relations with men must not be bought at the price of betraying her sisters (Sontag, 1973, p. 206).

To this I would add that from a truly feminist point of view these two responsibilities are inseparable.

I am curious to see what corresponding risks and self-confrontations men of intelligence and goodwill will be ready to undergo on behalf of women. It is one thing to have a single "exceptional" woman as your wife, daughter, friend, or protégé, or to long for a humanization of society by women; another to face each feminist issue—academic, social, personal—as it appears and to evade none. Many women who are not "man-haters" have felt publicly betrayed time and again by men on whose good faith and comradeship they had been relying on account of private conversations. I know that academic men are now hard-pressed for jobs and must fear the competition of women entering the university in greater numbers and with greater self-confidence. But masculine resistance to women's claims for full humanity is far more ancient, deeply rooted, and irrational than this year's job market. Misogyny should itself become a central subject of inquiry rather than continue as a desperate clinging to old, destructive fears and privileges. It will be interesting to see how many men are prepared to give more than rhetorical support today to the sex from which they have, for centuries, demanded and accepted so much.

If a truly universal and excellent network of child care can begin to develop, if women in sufficient numbers pervade the university at all levels—from community programs through college and professional schools to all ranks of teaching and administration—if the older, more established faculty women begin to get in touch with their (always, I am convinced) latent feminism, if even a few men come forward willing to think through and support feminist issues beyond their own immediate self-interest, there is a strong chance that in our own time we would begin to see some true "universality" of values emerging from the inadequate and distorted corpus of patriarchal knowlege. This will mean not a renaissance but a *nascence,* partaking of some inheritances from the past but working imaginatively far beyond them.

It is likely that in the immediate future various alternatives will be explored. Women's studies programs, where they are staffed by feminists, will serve as a focus for feminist values even in a patriarchal context. Even where staffed largely by tokenists, their very existence will make possible some rising consciousness in students. Already, alternate feminist institutes are arising to challenge the curriculum of established institutions.[12] Feminists may use the man-centered university as a base and resource while doing research and writing books and articles whose influence will be felt far beyond the academy. Consciously woman-centered universities—in which women shape the philosophy and the decision making though men may choose to study and teach there—may evolve from existing institutions.[13]

[12] For example, the Feminist Studio Workshop in Los Angeles, and the Sagaris Institute in Vermont.

[13] One formerly all-women's college, now coeducational, has recently attempted to define its woman-centeredness in relation to coeducation: "We recommend that for the foreseeable future Sarah Lawrence remain a college oriented towards the

Whatever the forms it may take, the process of women's repossession of ourselves is irreversible. Within and without academe, the rise in women's expectations has gone far beyond the middle-class and has released an incalculable new energy— not merely for changing institutions but for human redefinition; not merely for equal rights but for a new kind of being.

---

education of women. The women's movement, and the profound response it has elicited, makes it evident that institutions concerned with the particular needs and aspirations of women still have a vital place in American education. Without belittling the accomplishments of the women's colleges, including our own, we can now see that their influence operated in a subtly contradictory manner. Though they offered their students excellent training in the liberal and later the performing arts . . . the very character of that training reflected a patronizing view by the society-at-large—no doubt unconsciously reinforced by the institutions themselves—of the position of women. Because women were not expected to "do" anything with their education, it was assumed that they could devote themselves to the "useless" disciplines while most men were preparing themselves in their own enclave for the real business of life. The effect was to confirm the subordinate role of both women and liberal education in the American scheme of things. . . . A . . . worthwhile aim for a college oriented towards women would be to help them create out of themselves a framework of expectation that would escape stereotypes altogether. . . . Women must be encouraged to think in new ways about what to do with their lives.

"What this requires most of all is a college community aware of the problems of women and prepared to deal with these problems in the classroom and out. Since mature women obviously have a special role to play here, the college should make a maximum effort to hire and give support to women teachers and administrators—not necessarily those who have succeeded by conforming to male roles, but women whose exemplary struggle for autonomy may encourage young women to get beyond the fixed images of self that have been imposed on them. . . .

"We strongly support the Women's Studies Program. . . . We could not ask for a more appropriate means of dramatizing our commitment to the education of women than a program designed to make all students rethink the role of women in history . . ." (Sarah Lawrence College Report on Coeducation, 1973, pp. 1–2).

REFERENCES

American Sociological Association: *The Status of Women in Sociology,* Washington, D.C., 1973.

Beard, Mary: *Woman as Force in History,* Collier Books, The Macmillan Company, New York, 1971.

Bly, Robert: *Sleepers Joining Hands,* Harper & Row, Publishers, Incorporated, New York, 1973.

Brandeis University Bulletin, College of Arts and Sciences, Waltham, Mass., 1972–73.

Chesler, Phyllis: *Women and Madness,* Doubleday & Company, Inc., Garden City, New York, 1972.

Cross, Barbara M.: *The Educated Woman in America,* Teachers College Press, Columbia University, New York, 1965.

Cross, K. Patricia: "The Woman Student," in *Women in Higher Education,* American Council on Education, Washington, D.C., 1972.

Daly, Mary: *Beyond God the Father: Toward a Philosophy of Women's Liberation,* Beacon Press, Boston, 1973.

Ehrenreich, B., and D. English: *Witches, Midwives and Nurses: A History of Women Healers,* The Feminist Press, Old Westbury, N.Y., 1973.

Grimstad, K., and S. Rennie (eds.): *The New Woman's Survival Catalogue,* Coward, McCann and Geoghegan, New York, 1973.

Jacoby, Susan: "What Do I Do for the Next Twenty Years?" *New York Times Magazine,* June 17, 1973.

Kriegel, Leonard: *Working Through: A Teacher's Journey in the Urban University,* Saturday Review Press, New York, 1972.

Leffler, A., D. Gillespie, and E. Ratner: "Academic Feminists and the Women's Movement," *Ain't I A Woman?* vol. 4, no. 1, 1973.

Lifton, Robert J. (ed.): *The Woman in America,* Beacon Press, Boston, 1968.

Marcuse, Herbert: *Counterrevolution and Revolt,* Beacon Press, Boston, 1972.

Mendelsohn, Everett: "A Human Reconstruction of Science," prepared for *Women: Resource for a Changing World,* Radcliffe Institute Symposium, 1972; *Boston University Journal,* vol. 21, no. 2, Spring 1973.

Ong, Walter: "Review of Brian Vickers' *Classical Rhetoric in English Poetry,*" *College English,* February 1972.

Rank, Otto: *Beyond Psychology,* Dover Publications, Inc., New York, 1941.

Rees, Richard: *Simone Weil: A Sketch for a Portrait,* Oxford University Press, London, 1966.

Roby, Pamela (ed.): *Child Care: Who Cares?* Basic Books, Inc., Publishers, New York, 1973.

Rosaldo, M., and L. Lamphere: *Woman, Culture and Society,* Stanford University Press, Stanford, Calif., 1974.

Rosenfelt, Deborah (ed.): *Female Studies,* vol. 7, The Feminist Press, Old Westbury, N.Y., 1973.

Rossi, Alice S.: "Looking Ahead: Summary and Prospects," in Alice S. Rossi and Ann Calderwood (eds.), *Academic Women on the Move,* Russell Sage Foundation, New York, chap. 21, 1973.

Sarah Lawrence College Report on Coeducation, Apr. 9, 1973 (unpublished).

Shaughnessy, Mina P.: "Open Admissions and the Disadvantaged Teacher," keynote speech at the Conference on College Composition and Communication, New Orleans, April 1973 (unpublished).

Sicherman, Barbara: "The Invisible Woman," in *Women in Higher Education,* American Council on Education, Washington, D.C., 1972.

Sidel, Ruth: *Women and Child-Care in China,* Hill and Wang, Inc., New York, 1972.

Slater, Philip: *The Glory of Hera,* Beacon Press, Boston, 1968.

Slater, Philip: *The Pursuit of Loneliness,* Beacon Press, Boston, 1970.

Sontag, Susan: "The Third World of Women," *Partisan Review,* vol. 40, no. 2, 1973.

Woolf, Virginia: *Three Guineas,* Harcourt, Brace & World, Inc., New York, 1938, 1966.

2. Inside the Clockwork of Male Careers

by Arlie Russell Hochschild

An offhand remark made to me years ago has haunted me more and more ever since. I was talking at lunch with an acquaintance, and the talk turned, as it often does among women academicians just before it's time to part, to "how you manage" a full teaching schedule and family and how you feel about being a woman in a world of men. My acquaintance held a marginal position as one of two women in a department of fifty-five, a situation so common that I don't fear for her anonymity here. She said in passing, "My husband took our son to the university swimming pool the other day. He got so *embarrassed* being the only man with all those faculty wives and their kids." When the talk turned to her work, she said, "I was in a department meeting yesterday, and, you know, I always feel self-conscious. It's not that people aren't friendly . . . it's just that I feel I don't fit in." She felt "uneasy" in a world of men, he "embarrassed" in a world of women. It is not only the double world of swimming pools and department meetings that has haunted me, but his embarrassment, her unease.

This conversation recurred to me when I met with the Committee on the Status of Women, a newly formed senate committee on the Berkeley campus. We met in the Men's Faculty Club, a row of male scholars framing the dark walls, the waitresses bringing in coffee and taking out dishes. The talk was about discrimination and about the Affirmative Action Plan, a reluctant, ambiguous document that, to quote from its own elephant-foot language, "recognizes the desirability of removing obstacles to the flow of ability into appropriate occupational roles."

The well-meaning biologist on the committee was apologizing for his department, the engineer reminding us that they were "looking very hard" for a woman and a black, and another reminding us that things were getting better all the time. But I

47

remember feeling what many of us probably sensed but didn't say: that an enormously complex problem—one world of swimming pools, children, and women, and another of men in departments and committee meetings—that an overwhelming reality was being delicately sliced into the tiny tidbits a giant bureaucracy could digest. I wondered if anything in that Affirmative Action Plan, and others like it across the country, would begin to merge these double worlds. What such plans ignore is that fact that the existing academic career subcontracts work to the family—work women perform. Without changing the structure of this career, and its imperial relation to the family, it will be impossible for married women to move up in careers and for men to move into the family.

I would like to start by asking a simple and familiar question: Why, at a public university like the University of California at Berkeley in 1972, do women compose 41 percent of the entering freshmen, 37 percent of the graduating seniors, 31 percent of the applicants for admission to graduate school, 28 percent of the graduate admissions, 24 percent of the doctoral students, 21 percent of advanced doctoral students, 12 percent of Ph.D.'s, 38 percent of instructors, 9 percent of assistant professors, 6 percent of associate professors, and 3 percent of full professors (Ervin-Tripp, 1973)? This classic pattern is typical for women at all major universities, and the situation in nearly all of them is, as in Berkeley, worse than it was in 1930 (Graham, 1971).

I have heard two standard explanations for this classic pattern, but I doubt that either gets to the bottom of the matter. One explanation is that the university discriminates against women. If only tomorrow it could halt discrimination and become an impartial meritocracy, there would be many more academic women. The second explanation is that women are trained early to avoid success and authority and, lacking good role models as well, they "cool themselves out."

Since we already have some excellent and up-to-date objective studies[1] addressed to this question, in this essay I shall try to

---

[1] See Alice S. Rossi and Ann Calderwood (eds.), *Academic Women on the Move* (1973); Susan Mitchell, *Women and the Doctorate* (1968); and a publication based on the recent massive survey sponsored by the Carnegie Commission: Saul Feldman, *Escape from the Doll's House: Women in Graduate and Professional School Education* (1974). See also Carnegie Commission on Higher Education, *Opportunities for Women in Higher Education* (1973).

explore my own experience, comparing it occasionally to findings in other studies, in order to explain why a third explanation rings more true to me: namely, that the classic profile of the academic career is cut to the image of the traditional man with his traditional wife. To ask why more women are not full professors, or "full" anything else in the upper reaches of the economy, we have to ask first what it means to be a male full professor—socially, morally, and humanly—and what kind of system makes them into what they become.

The academic career is founded on some peculiar assumptions about the relation between doing work and competing with others, competing with others and getting credit for work, getting credit and building a reputation, building a reputation and doing it while you're young, doing it while you're young and hoarding scarce time, hoarding scarce time and minimizing family life, minimizing family life and leaving it to your wife— the chain of experiences that seems to anchor the traditional academic career. Even if the meritocracy worked perfectly, even if women did not cool themselves out, I suspect there would remain in a system that defines careers this way only a handful of women at the top.

If Machiavelli had turned his pen, as so many modern satirists have, to how a provincial might come to the university and become a full professor, he might have the following advice: enter graduate school with the same mentality with which you think you will emerge from graduate school. Be confident, ambitious, and well-aimed. Don't waste time. Get a good research topic early and find an important but kindly and nonprejudicial benefactor from whom you actually learn something. Most important, put your all into those crucial years after you get your doctorate—in your twenties and thirties—putting nothing else first then. Take your best job offer and go there no matter what your family or social situation. Publish your first book with a well-known publisher, and cross the land to a slightly better position, if it comes up. Extend your now-ambitious self broadly and deeply into research, committee work, and editorships, to make your name in your late twenties and at the latest early thirties. If somewhere along the way teaching becomes the psychic equivalent of volunteer work, don't let it bother you. You are now a full professor and can guide other young fledglings along that course.

Perhaps I am caricaturing, but bear in mind that I am talking about why only 4 percent of the full professors are women at universities like Berkeley, where I think it is fair to say this describes the cardboard outline of the "ideal" career. Ideals are the measuring rods of experience. Even if, as a moral dropout, a student rejects this ideal, he or she finds himself or herself nonetheless in competition with others who rise to the top to exemplify and uphold the ideal.

But there is something hidden in the description of this academic career: the family. And at present men and women have different ties to the family. I think this is not accidental, for the university (a comparatively flexible institution at that) seeks to immunize itself against the vicissitudes of human existence that are out of its control. Some of these vicissitudes are expressed and absorbed in the family: birth at one end of the life cycle and death at the other. Lower ages at retirement handle the "problem" of death, and the exclusion of women the "problem" of birth. (If it could, the university would also guard against other human traumas, sickness, insanity, postdivorce depression, now removed from it by sabbaticals and leaves of absence.) The family is in some sense a preindustrial institution and lives in a private, more flexible time, remote from the immortal industrial clock. The family absorbs vicissitudes that the workplace discards.

It is the university's welfare agency, and women are its social workers. That is to say, the family serves a function for the university, and at present women have more to do with the family than men. As a result, Machiavelli's advice suits them less well. Women Ph.D.'s in the United States spend about 28 hours per week on household tasks (Graham, 1971). Also, the twenties and sometimes the thirties are normally a time to bear and raise children. But it is at precisely this stage that one begins to hear talk about "serious contribution to the field" and "reputation," which are always more or less promising than those of another of one's age. The result is apparent from a glance at a few crucial details cemented to her curriculum vita: How long did she take for the degree? Full-time, continuous work? Previous jobs, the best she could get? But the result shows too in how she sees herself in a career. For most academic women have been socialized at least twice, once to be women (as housewives and mothers) and once again to be like men (in traditional careers).

The second socialization raises the issue of *assimilation* to the male culture associated with academic life; the first socialization raises the issue of what women abandon in the process. The question we must unbury lies between the first socialization and the second: How much do women want careers to change them and how much do women want to change careers?

DISCRIMINATION   When I entered Berkeley as a graduate student in 1962, I sat with some fifty other incoming students that first week in a methodology course. One of the two sociology professors on the podium before us said, "We say this to every incoming class and we'll say it to you. Look to your left and look to your right. Two out of three of you will drop out before you are through, probably in the first two years." We looked blankly to right and left, and quick nervous laughter jumped out and back from the class. I wonder now, a decade later, what each of us was thinking at that moment. I remember only that I didn't hear a word during the rest of the hour, for wondering whether it would be the fellow on my left, or the one on my right, or me. A fifth of my incoming class was female, and in the three years that followed, indeed, three-quarters of the women (and half of the men) did drop out.[2] But a good many neither dropped out nor moved on, but stayed trapped between the M.A. and the orals, or the orals and the dissertation, fighting the private devil of a writing block, or even relaxing within that ambiguous passage, like those permanent "temporary buildings" still standing on the Berkeley campus since World War II. Some even developed a humor to counter the painful jokes about them: "What do you have in your briefcase there, samples?"

[2] Where did these women go? Several I knew stopped their degrees—trying to find a way to continue—to follow their men where military service, schooling, or work took them, or to have children, or to work while their husbands continued their studies. One woman dropped out of a later class more flamboyantly, writing a notice that stayed for a long time on the blackboard of the graduate student lounge, a reminder to buy her avocado and bean-sprout sandwiches at a small stall on Sproul Hall plaza.

A recent Decennial Report from the Harvard and Radcliffe College Class of 1963 contained essays about what had happened to people since their graduation, many like the following: "We have moved from NYC to the mountains above Boulder . . . a very happy change. Dan is teaching math at Colorado University and I continue slow progress on my dissertation while waiting for another baby in May, and caring for Ben, already very much with us."

This happens to men, too, but why does it happen so much more to women? According to some analysts, the women leave academe because of discrimination in such matters as getting fellowships, job offers, or promotions. Helen Astin (1969), for example, concludes that this is a major reason, citing the fact that a full third of the women Ph.D.'s she studied reported discrimination. Others, such as Jessie Bernard, suggest that "it is only when *other* grounds for rejection are missing that prejudiced discrimination *per se* is brought into play" (Bernard, 1966, p. 49). I suspect that Bernard is more on the mark. While a third of academic women reporting discrimination is a great number, it is also remarkable that two-thirds did not report it.

Much of the discrimination argument rests on how broadly we define discrimination or how trained the eye is for "seeing" it. Women have acclimatized themselves to discrimination, expect it, get it, and try to move around it. It is hard to say, since I continually re-remember those early years through different prisms, whether I experienced any discrimination myself. I don't think so, unless one counts the time I entered a professor's office to discuss my paper topic for his course. We had been assigned a reading that involved the link between a particular phenomenon and social class. Social class was measured, I had learned, by the Hollingshead and Redlich index of social class. Somewhere along in the interview, in the course of explaining the paper I was hoping to write, I was pretentious enough to mention the Hollingshead and Redlich index, which involves education, occupational prestige, and residence. The professor stopped me dead with a stony gaze. "Are you a *graduate* student?" (not an *under*graduate). It was like a punch in the stomach, and it took me a few seconds to recover.[3] The interview traveled on as if this exchange had never occurred and I left the office, with a lump in my throat, went to the women's bathroom, and cried. I blush now at my anxiety to please. But of course the problem was not that I was too pretentious, but that I did it badly. In the many

---

[3] Feldman's data suggest that in those fields where 30 to 50 percent of the students are female—and sociology is among these—40 percent of the males and 50 percent of the females said the professor closest to them viewed them "as a student," or else had no contact with them outside the classroom. Sixty percent of the males and 49 percent of the females said their closest professor viewed them "as a colleague," or "as an apprentice" (recomputed from Feldman, 1974, table 33, pp. 92–93).

imaginary rehearsals of second encounters (I never went back), the conversation went like this: "Hollingshead and Redlich index, mmmmmmm, it's better than the old Warner index, of course, but then it misses some of the more sophisticated indicators of the Chapin scale, dated as it is." By the time it occurred to me that the *man's* occupation and education were taken as predictors of the social class of his wife and children, I stopped imagining conversations with this particular person.

In the recent Carnegie survey of 32,000 graduate students and faculty, 22 percent of the men and 50 percent of the women graduate students in sociology agreed that the faculty does not "take female graduate students seriously," and in fact a quarter of the male faculty and 3.6 percent of the female faculty agreed that "female graduate students are not as dedicated to the field as males" (Feldman, 1974, p. 71).

When the graduate students were asked the same question, a quarter—men and women alike—agreed that "women are not as dedicated." Only the female *faculty* refused to be recorded this way, perhaps feeling as I did when I filled out the questionnaire that there was no place to say between the yes and the no, that dedication has to be measured against the visible or felt incentives to go on, and that lack of dedication may be a defensive anticipation of being ignored.

For women in particular the line between dropping out, staying on, and moving out is a thin and fluctuating one. The Carnegie Commission study asked graduate students, "Have you ever considered in the past year quitting graduate school for good?" Only 43 percent of the women and 53 percent of the men had *not* considered it (Sells, forthcoming doctoral dissertation).[4] I considered it to the extent of interviewing at the end of my first miserable year for several jobs in New York that did not pan out. Beyond that, my uncertainty expressed itself in virtually every paper I wrote for the first two years. I can hardly read the papers now since it appears that for about a year and a half I never changed the typewriter ribbon. As one professor wrote on a paper, "Fortunately the writer's exposition and analysis are a pleasant contrast to a manuscript which in physical appearance

---

[4] There were more (39 percent) single women than men (29 percent), and 43 percent of the single women and 61 percent of single men did not consider dropping out in the last year.

promises the worst. A nice job of comparing Condorcet and Rousseau. . . . The writer would possibly have profited by . . . more systematically *resolving* [sic] at least tentatively the problem raised—for purposes of relieving her own apparent ambivalence on the issue." I am less sure now that it was Condorcet and Rousseau I was ambivalent about.

That ambivalence centered, I imagine, on a number of issues, but one of them was probably the relation between the career I might get into and the family I might have. I say "probably" because I didn't see it clearly that way, for I saw nothing very clearly then.

The categorical judgments that powerful people apply to particular women are often justified on the grounds that family comes first. Now we call these judgments "discrimination." One chairman caught in print before 1967 said what many department chairmen probably still think but no longer say:

My own practice is to appoint women to about 50 percent of our graduate assistantships and to about 30 percent of our instructorships. My fear that this is too large a proportion of women appointees arises from the considerations: (1) that women are less likely to complete the degree programs upon which they embark; (2) that even if they do, marriage is very likely to intervene and to prevent or considerably delay their entry into the teaching profession; (3) that even when they do become full time teachers . . . their primary sense of responsibility is to their homes, so that they become professional only to a limited degree; (4) that they are far less likely than men to achieve positions of leadership in their profession (Bernard, 1966, p. 43).

Such official judgments are not completely absurd. They rest on empirical evidence of *categorical* differences between men and women, regardless of special exceptions. To ignore this fact does not make it go away. In ignoring it, we also seem tacitly to agree with university officials that the family is, after all, a private matter out of official hands. It prevents us from asking whether there isn't something about the academic system itself that perpetuates this "private" inequality.

WOMEN COOLING THEMSELVES OUT The second explanation for the attrition of women in academe touches private inequality more directly: women sooner or later cool themselves out by a form of "autodiscrimination." Here, inequality is conceived not as the mark of a chairperson's pen, but as the consequence of a whole constellation of dis-advantages.

It is admittedly hard to distinguish between women who remove themselves from the university and women who are removed or who are moved *to* remove themselves. For there are innumerable aspects of graduate school that are not quite discriminatory and not quite not discriminatory either. Some things are simply *discouraging:* the invisibility of women among the teachers and writers of the books one reads or among the faces framed on the walls of the faculty club; the paucity of women at the informal gathering over beer after the seminar. Then there are the prelecture jokes (to break the ice) that refer in some way to pretty girls as a distraction, or to getting into "virginal" fields.[5] There is also the continual, semiconscious work of sensing and avoiding professors who are known to dislike or discredit women or particular types of women. Even the stress on mathematics in sociology: one professor in my department seriously suggested the adding of stiffer methodology requirements in order to reduce the number of women undergraduate majors. In addition, there is the low standing of the "female" specialties—like sociology of the family and education—which some early feminists like me scrupulously avoided for that stupid reason. The real thing to study, of course, was political sociology and general theory: those were virtually all-male classes, from which one could emerge with a "command" of the important literature.

Women are discouraged by competition and by the need to be, despite their training, unambivalent about ambition. Ambition is no static or given thing, like having blue eyes. It is more like sexuality, variable, subject to influence, and attached to past loves, deprivations, rivalries, and the many events long erased from memory. Some people would be ambitious anywhere, but competitive situations tend to drive ambition underground in women. Despite supportive mentors, for many women there still remains something intangibly frightening about a competitive environment, competitive seminar talk, even about argumentative writing. While feminists have challenged the fear of competition—both by competing successfully and by refusing to compete—and while some male dropouts crossing over the other way

---

[5] It is often said that feminists lack a sense of humor. Actually it's that after discovering the joke is on us, we've developed a different one.

advise against competing, the issue is hardly settled for most women. For those who cannot imagine themselves inside a competitive environment, the question becomes: How much is something wrong with me and how much is something wrong with my situation?

MODELS OF PEOPLE AND PLACES It is often said that a good female "role model" can make up for the pervasive discouragement women find in academe. By role model I mean simply a person whom a student feels she wants to be like or could become. It is someone she may magically incorporate into herself, someone who, intentionally or not, throws her a psychic lifeline. A role model is thus highly personal and idiosyncratic, although she may nonetheless fit a social pattern. I am aware of being part of an invisible parade of models. Even as I seek a model myself, I partly am one to students who are, in turn, models to still others. Various parades of role models crisscross each other in the university, and each goes back in psychological time.

For example, I distinctly remember my mother directing me at the age of 16 toward a model of a professional woman who had followed her husband from place to place outside the United States. My mother worked hard in support of my father's work in the foreign service, and while her own situation did not permit her a career, it was something she had always admired. At one cocktail party, crowded and noisy, she whispered in my ear, "Mrs. Cohen. Go talk to Mrs. Cohen. She's a *doctor*, you know." I hesitated, not knowing what I could say or ask. My mother made eye signs and I ventured over to Mrs. Cohen. As it turned out, she was the hostess of the party. One of her three small children was complaining that he couldn't unlock his bicycle. A tray of hors d'oeuvres had spilled and Mrs. Cohen was hysterical. She was ignoring her son and the spilled hors d'oeuvres for the moment and concentrated on stuffing some eggs, every fifth one of which she ate. As I began preparing the eggs with her, she explained why practicing psychiatry outside the country was impossible, that moving every two years messed up the relations she might have had with her patients, had she any patients. She popped yet another egg into her mouth and disappeared into the crowd. Yes, Mrs. Cohen was a model of something, the best model my mother could find for me, and only now do I begin to understand her situation and my mother's.

Actually it was not so much Dr. Cohen herself as it was her whole life, as part of what Hanna Papanek (1973) calls the "two person career" that became, for me, the negative model. I imagine that 20 years from now, young women will, in the same way, scan individual models to sense the underlying situation, the little imperialisms of a man's career on his wife's life. Dr. Cohen's husband had one role and his role created two for her. Male careers in other fields, including academe, differ from this only in degree.

This is the second sense in which we can talk of models—models of *situations* that allow a woman to be who she gradually gets to want to be. Models of people and of situations, some appealing and some distressing, march silently across the university grounds. Among the inspiring leaders of this parade are also some frightening examples of women who lack the outer symbolic or material rewards for accomplishment: the degrees, the higher-level jobs, the promotions, the grants that their male counterparts have. In some cases too these women show the inner signs: a creativity that may have cramped itself into modest addenda, replications of old research, or reformations of some man's theory—research, in sum, that will not "hurt anyone's feeling." What is painful is not simply that a particular woman may have been denied a job, but rather, that she may face the daily experience of being labeled a dull or unpromising dutiful daughter in research. The human pinch for such a woman is not simply having to choose between a full-time commitment to her profession or a family, but what it means to remain single among couples, to have her sexual life an item of amused curiosity. For others it isn't simply the harried life of trying to work and raise a family at the same time; it's the premature aging around the eyes, the third drink at night, the tired resignation when she opens the door to a sparkling freshman who wants to know "all about how social science can cure the world of war and poverty."[6] There are other kinds of models, too. Especially in recent years, women have earned degrees and good jobs and with it all

---

[6] I do not define those women as oppressed who *think* they are or have been. Some are declaratively self-conscious and others not, and they may be variously analytical and insightful about the effects of personal and institutional sexism. On the whole, among older women academics, I think a "Protestant" cultural style of dealing with oppression prevails, according to which it is unseemly to be long-suffering or indeed to have any problems at all that show. The "Catholic" or "Jewish" cultural styles, according to which it is more legitimate to openly acknowledge pain, are at least nowadays more appropriate.

have established egalitarian arrangements at home. But I think they are likely to remain a minority because of the current tight job market and the career system itself and because women inside academe are often constrained from lobbying for more women. It's not *professional.* Speaking only for myself, I have found it extremely hard to lobby for change, to politic while sitting in a department meeting with dozens of senior male professors, among them my mentors. I have felt like a totem or representative more than an agent of social change, discredited for being that by some professors and for not being more than that by some feminists. Of course when I do speak up, it is with all too much feeling. It is immeasurably easier, a joyous release, to go to the private turf of my classroom where I become intellectually and morally bold. If I had to locate what has been my own struggle, it would be right there in the committee room.

Women respond not simply to a psychological lifeline in the parade, but to the social ecology of survival. If we are to talk about good models we must talk about the context that produces them. To ignore this is to risk running into the problems I did when I accepted my first appointment as the first woman sociologist in a small department at the University of California at Santa Cruz. Some very strange things happened to me, but I am not so sure that anything happened to the department or university. Sprinkled thinly as women were across departments there, we created a new minority status where none had existed before, models of token women. The first week there, I began receiving Xeroxed newspaper clippings and magazine articles praising the women's movement or detailing how bad the "woman situation" was in medicine or describing Danish women dentists. These clippings that began to swell my files were invariably attached to a friendly forwarding note: "Thought you'd be interested," or "Just saw this and thought of you." I stopped an older colleague in the hall to thank him for an article he had given me and inquired what he had thought of it. He hadn't read it himself. I began to realize that I was becoming my colleagues' friendly totem, a representation of feminism. "I'm all with you people" began to seem more like "You be it for us." And sure enough. But for every paper I read on the philosophy of Charlotte Gilman, on the history of the garment union, the dual career family, or women and art, I wondered if I shouldn't poke a copy into the mailboxes of my clipping-sending friends. I had wound myself into a feminist cocoon and left the tree standing serenely as it was. No, it takes more than this kind of "model."

THE CLOCKWORK OF THE CAREER SYSTEM It is not easy to clip and press what I am talking about inside the square boundaries of an "administrative problem." The context has to do with the very clockwork of a career system that seems to eliminate women not so much through malevolent disobedience to good rules, but through making up rules to suit half the population in the first place.[7] For all the turmoil of the 1960s, those rules have not changed a bit. The year 1962 was an interesting one to come to Berkeley, and 1972 a depressing one. The free speech movement in 1964 and the black power and women's liberation movements following it seem framed now by the fifties and Eisenhower on one side and the seventies, Nixon, and Ford on the other. The questions that lay flat under the book in the lecture hall in 1963 stood up to declare themselves in that stubborn public square that refused to be incorporated by the city-state around it. It was like slicing the *Queen Mary* in half: from boiler room to top deck, the chains of command within, the ties to industry and the military without, in what had announced itself as an otherworldly search for Truth—all were exposed for a moment in history. And then recovered, the boat a whole again and set afloat. It was what did *not* change that was most impressive. Now FSM, black power, and women's liberation appear as dissertation topics: "FSM, a Study of Information Dissemination," "Black Power as Status Mobility," "The Changing Image of Career Women," amidst yet newer ones such as "In the Service of Light; a Sociological Essay on the Knowledge of Guru Maharaj Ji and the Experience of His Devotees." Each movement left a theater of its own, and frosted dinner-table conversations that at the end of the evening divided again by sex.

[7] In what follows, I focus on the problems for women of the career system, assuming that the virtues of academe make it worth criticizing. Perhaps I need not say that few people love their work as much as professors do, and I, too, can genuinely not imagine a more engrossing and worthwhile life than one devoted to discovering how the world works and inspiring an appreciation for culture and inquiry. But this essay is not about why women should be in the university, but an essay about why they are not.

What did not change was the career system, brilliantly described by Clark Kerr in *The Uses of the University* (Kerr, 1963). But there are some things about competition uncritically implied in that book that I must focus on here. The first is the understanding, taken for granted, that work is shaped into a "career" and that a "career" comprises a series of positions and accomplishments, each of which is tightly and competitively measured against other careers, so that even minor differences in achievement count. Universities and departments compete to get the "big names," and individuals compete to become the people who are competed for. There is competition between Berkeley and Harvard, between Stony Brook and New York University, between sociology and history, between this assistant professor and that one, the competition trickling down from level to level. The people at each level carefully inspect the relatively minor differences between a surprisingly narrow band of potential rivals for scarce but coveted rewards. This is perhaps more apparent in the almost-famous than the famous universities, and in the hard sciences, whose scientists have more to sell (and sell out), than in the soft. It is more apparent at professional conventions than in the classroom, more in graduate student talk than in undergraduate, more among males than females. The career itself is based on a series of contests, which in turn are based not so much on doing good work as on getting *credit* for doing good work.

This was explained to me by a colleague in a letter. (I had written him asking why employers are not more enthusiastic about part-time work for men and women.) Speaking about scientific and artistic creativity, he notes:

. . . being the first to solve some problems helps you be the first to solve a problem which depends on the solution of the first (intellectual problem), *provided* that you get to work on the second problem before everybody learns how you solved the first. I think clienteles work pretty much the same way, that if you start being known as a good doctor in a certain social circle, or a good divorce lawyer, then if two of the person's friends recommend you as a good professional you are much more likely to get his business than if only one does. Where clienteles come in off the street or in response to advertisements, as in real estate, then it doesn't matter so much whether you work full time or not. . . .

"Being the first" to solve the problem is not, under the career system, the same as getting the problem solved; "getting his business" away from someone else is not the same as meeting the client's needs. In the university, this means "being the first" in research and, to a much lesser extent, "getting the business" in teaching. To borrow from movement language, one can manage in this way to get a reputation in the "star system." Wanting to become a "star," or knowing you have to want to become one, or becoming even a minor one, is what women learn in man-made careers.

A reputation is measured against time—that is, against the year one is born. A number of studies have shown that, in modern times, intellectual achievements tend to come surprisingly early in life. In Harvey Lehman's massive study of eminent men in science, the arts, letters, politics, the military, and the judiciary, the average age of peak performance is early: for chemists and physicists the early thirties, in music and sculpture the late thirties, even in philosophy the late thirties and early forties. The link between age and achievement for many specialties housed in the university resembles that of athletes more than that of popes or judges. Interestingly, achievement came later in life for men before 1775—before the massive bureaucratization of work into the career system (Lehman, 1953, 1962, 1965). A reputation is an imaginary promise to the world that if one is productive young in life, one will be so later also. And the university, having little else to go on, rewards the promise of the young or fairly young.

Age discrimination is not some separate extra unfairness thoughtlessly tacked on to universities; it follows inevitably from the bottommost assumptions about university careers. If jobs are scarce and promising reputations important, who wants a 50-year-old mother of three with a dissertation almost completed? Since age is the measure of achievement, competition often takes the form of working long hours[8] and working harder than the next person. This definition of work does not refer to teaching, committee work, office hours, phone conversations with students, editing students' work, but refers more narrowly to one's

---

[8] Not all competition can be explained in these terms, but it may partly explain why some occupational groups work longer hours than others. For example, we find among managers, officials, and proprietors, that 27 percent of males in 1970 worked 60 hours or more per week, while only 2 percent of clerical workers worked that hard. Self-employed workers, such as farm managers, work harder than employees. In large bureaucracies, it tends to be those at or near the top who work the longest hours—the careerists.

own work. Time becomes a scarce resource that one hoards greedily, and time becomes the thing one talks about when one is wasting it. If "doing one's work" is a labor of love, love itself comes to have an economic and honorific base.

This conception of time becomes in turn an indelible part of the career-*self*.[9] Male-styled careers introduce women to a new form of time consciousness: it is not age measured against beauty, as in our "first" training, but age measured against achievement. That measure of age, as I have noted, is related to what else a person does, for example, in the family.

The career-self experiences time as linear and the career itself as a measured line, other parts of the self following along. Time is objectified in the academic vita, which grows longer with each article and book, and not with each vegetable garden, camping trip, political meeting, or child. One's multifold potential is treated much like a capital investment in an initially marginal enterprise. What is won for the garden is lost to the vita. For the career-self, casual comparisons to colleagues working on the same problem are magnified into contests: He got his article published first. His good news is my bad news. These comparisons become mental giants, while the rest of the world and self are experientially dwarfed.

If work, conceptualized as a career, becomes a measured line, the line often appears to be a rising one. Very often the rising career line is also, despite a residual cynicism about power, associated with a pleasant belief in the progress of the world. Even those who have refused to fit this profile know very well that they are measured against it by others who rise to the top and, from this top-of-the-career world view, set the prevailing standards.

THE SOCIAL PSYCHOLOGY OF CAREER TALK The academic career creates a culture of its own, and a special sense of self. This is especially true for the elite and aspirants to it, but it holds for the stragglers and misfits as well. The marketplace is not somewhere "out there" in the great beyond of

[9] Some of the ideas presented here come from reading Dorothy Lee's *Freedom and Culture* (1965), a study of American Indians and a book that forces one to rethink the concept of the individual *versus* society, a favored antagonism of Western sociologists. The Wintu Indians, whom she describes, do not conceptualize a "self" upon which to base a career; the very concept of self does not have a meaning in their tribal configuration, and there is no word in the language corresponding to it.

supply and demand; it insinuates itself into the very fiber of human communication about things that matter.

Apart from writing, the main thing academics do is talk, and talk is perhaps the best illustration of the effects of this culture. Talk anywhere is influenced by the context in which it goes on, and I should say a little about that. If a Cuban or a Wintu Indian happened to walk down the fourth floor of Barrows Hall at Berkeley, she might get the impression of a bare mustard yellow tunnel, long and dimly lit from above, casting ghostly shadows on the under-eyes of its "trespassers." Closed doors to left and right offer a few typed notices of class meeting schedules, envelopes containing graded examinations, and one wry sign, posted several months earlier by a man who had just won tenure: THIS MACHINE IS NOT IN ORDER. It might be experienced as a place where no one lives. It's the one place professors are supposed to be available to students, but since students unwittingly block the extension of one's vita, it's the one place from which professors are curiously absent. Only instructors not yet in the tenure race and older professors on the other side of it might answer to a knock. The rest are seemingly lost between their several offices (the institute, the department, the home). Often they pick up their mail at dawn or dusk when the department office is closed. The French call them the "hurried class." On a day when the printed notice says a middle-rank professor will be in, a small society of students will assemble on the floor against one wall. They have penciled their names on a posted sheet that marks time in 15-minute pieces; and they may be rehearsing their lines.

Last term a male graduate student signed up for an office visit. On my office door, in large, bold letters he wrote: THOMPSON. That the name was larger than the others led me to expect a large, imposing figure. In fact, Thompson was 3 inches shorter than I, and I suppose he felt less imposing as well. For after he had seated himself carefully, slowly crossed his legs, and hunched down in the "student" chair, he began, without prodding on my part, to give a long, slow description of his intellectual evolution from mathematical models at the University of Michigan to historical sociology to possibly, just possibly— and this was why he was in my office—the sociology of the family. It took about half an hour to say. The remarkable thing was how slowly and deliberately he spoke, as if he were dictating a manuscript, qualifying each statement, painfully footnoting his generalizations, and offering summaries at the appropriate places, rather like the chairman of our department. After the interview was concluded, with a fumble over who should open the door (Whose door knob was it? Is he a student or a man? Am I a woman or a professor?), I could hear THOMPSON behind me, talking with a graduate student friend, in a brisk, conversational dialogue, laughing a bit and even rambling. He was talking in a dramatically different way—normally. He wasn't selling smartness to a professor.

THOMPSON thought he was being judged in that interview against other graduate students. And he was right. Every month or two I do receive a confidential form from my department, asking me to rank from mediocre to excellent a series of 10 to 20 graduate students. Professors are the last people most students come to with an intellectual problem, and the first people they come to when they have solved it. To expose their vulnerability or confusion is to risk being marked "mediocre" on the confidential form.

The culture of the career system is not, alas, confined to the office interview. Despite the signs of otherworldliness, the Volvos and blue-jean patches and beards, the university is a market world, a world of conspicuous consumption. It is not gold brooches and Cadillacs that are conspicuously consumed; it is intellectual talk. I sometimes get the impression in the corridor outside my office, at dinner parties, and in countless meetings, that vita is talking to vita, that tenure is being won in a conversational tournament, that examinations have slipped out of their end-of-semester slots and entered the walls and ceiling and floor of talk. The intellectual dozens, Leonard Kriegel calls them in his book *Working Through.* It is academic street-corner talk at which one is informally tracked as excellent, good, fair, poor, or terrible. If you bring someone out (as women are taught to do) instead of crowding him out, you get bad marks. Not to learn to talk this way at this place is like living without a skin; it is a required language.

It is often said that women do not speak up in class as much as men do, and I have noticed it, too, occasionally even in my graduate seminar on the sociology of sex roles. The reason, I suspect, is that they are aware that they have not yet perfected the proper style.(It is often older women, not yet aware of the stylistic requirements, who speak up.) Some say also that women are ignored in conversation because they are sex objects; I think, rather, that they are defined as conversational cheerleaders to the verbal tournament.

The verbal tournament seems also to require a socially shared negativism toward other people's work. It is often considered an evening well spent, for example, to tear down Merton's theory of anomie, or to argue that Susan Sontag is overrated, that Erving Goffman is passé, that Noam Chomsky's latest article, like most other things one has read lately, says nothing really new. It is as if from these collective wreckings of intellectual edifices the participants will emerge, in some small way, larger. But the negative talk about the stupidity of academic conversations, the drivel in the *American Sociological Review,* which one proudly claims not to have read in two years, also establishes a social floor of civility, a silent pact to be friends or associates, regardless of one's rise or fall in market value. In a sad way, it says, "Despite the gridded walls around us, you and I share *something* in common after all."

There is still another kind of talk, not in one's private office, or in the halls, and rarely at parties, but in the main office: faculty talk to secretaries. That talk generally is brief, smiley, and rich with campus gossip, news of the Xerox machine, or good places to eat. It obeys the rules of civility and obscures the irritations or jealousies that might momentarily stop work. It also tends to foster the secretaries' identification with the professorial career. We happen in my department to have a "liberated" secretarial pool, who see this kind of talk through a feminist prism as condescending and manipulative, a sort of oil and grease of the machinery that maintains a pay and status for them far below what an early estimate of potential would have predicted. Unable to change their essential condition, they jealously guard their poster of a Vietnamese woman on the wall in the main office, and have given up smiling to any who daily invade their public space, they having no private space at all. Their new model of talk is that between a union negotiator and the business representative. Here it's not vita talking to vita, but worker talking to boss, be it man or (the assimilated) woman. The administration considers the secretarial pool a "problem," but their new style is more basically a challenge not only to their inferior status, but to what about talk holds them in place.

Women compromise with the career culture in various ways. It is as common among women as it is among men to consider market talk gauche—who got what job, was awarded what grant, or had an article accepted by which journal. On the other hand, a woman is "unserious" or fuzzy-headed if she appears to be out of it altogether. The compromise some women effect is to publicly endorse anticompetitive or noncompetitive values, while privately practicing the competitive ones. One publicly discredits the "rat race" and then, at home on weekends, climbs quietly onto the revolving wheel.

Academic talk reflects academic life and academic life reflects a marketplace. Ideas become products that are "owned" or "borrowed" or "stolen" from their owners, products that through talk and in print rise and fall in market value, and products that have become alienated from their producers. The marketplace pervades the life of conservatives and radicals alike, for whom ideas are still "products." Even if, with the growth of giant monopolies, the country *as a whole* is no longer capitalist in the old-fashioned sense, in a peculiar way the university, especially for its junior members, is.

I suspect that a different system would produce a different talk. And women trained to this career unwittingly learn to admire in others and perfect in themselves the talk that goes with the system—for it is uncompetitive, undressed, nonproduct, supportive talk that is, in the last analysis, discriminated against.

Even writing about career talk in cynical language, I find that, bizarrely enough, I don't *feel* cynical, even while I think that way; and I have tried to consider why. I think it is because I know, in a distant corner of my mind, that the very impersonality that competition creates provides the role of the "humanizer" that I so enjoy filling. I know that only in a hierarchy built on fear (it's called "respect," but that is an emotional alloy with a large part of fear in it) is there a role for those who reduce it. Only in a conservative student body is there a role for the "house radical." Only in a department with no women are you considered "really something" to be the first. A bad system ironically produces a market, on its underside, for the "good guys." I know this, but it somehow does not stop me from loving to teach. For it is from this soft spot, in the underbelly of the whale, that a counteroffensive can begin against women's second socialization to career talk and all that goes with it.

The links between competition, career, reputation, and time consciousness extend to life that is at once outside the university but inside the career culture: that is, to the family and to the faculty wife. The university has no *formal* administrative policy toward the families of its members. I have never heard of the university equivalent to the "farming out system" in early industry, or of families being brought into the university the way they were taken into nineteenth-century factories. Certainly we do not hear of a family winning a Ford Foundation grant, aunts and uncles doing the interviewing, husband and wife the analysis and writing, leaving footnotes to the children. While books have been typed, if not partly written, by wives, the family in the university has never been the productive *unit* of it.

Nonetheless, I think we have what amounts to a tacit policy toward the family. Let us consider the following: *if all else were equal,* who would be most likely to survive under the career system—a man married to a full-time housewife and mother; or a man whose wife has a nine-to-five job and the children in day care; or a man who works part-time, as does his wife, while their children are small? I think the general principle that determines the answer is this: *To the extent that his family (1) does not positively help him in his work or (2) makes demands on his time and psychic energy that compete with those devoted to his job, they lower his chances for survival. This is true insofar as he is competing with other men whose wives either aid them or do not interfere with their work.* Other things being equal, the university rewards the married family-free man.

But intellectual productivity is sometimes discussed as if it were a gift from heaven to the chosen few, which had nothing to do with families or social environment at all. If we inspect the social context of male productivity, we often find nameless women and a few younger men feeding the "productive one" references, computer outputs, library books, and cooked dinners. Women, single or married, are in competition not simply with men, but with the *heads* of *small branch industries.*

A few book prefaces tell the familiar story. A book on racial oppression written in 1972:

Finally, I would like to thank my wife _____, who suffered the inconveniences that protracted writing brought about with as much graciousness as could be expected, and who instructed our children, _____ and _____, to respect the privacy of their father's work.

An earlier book, 1963: In many ways my wife Suzanne should be coauthor. She shared the problems of planning and carrying out the field work, and the life of a wife-mother-interviewer in another culture was more demanding than either of us might have imagined. Although she did not take part in the actual writing, she has been a patient sounding board, and her concern with individual cases provided a needed balance to my irrepressible desire to paint the broad picture.

Still one more, 1962: _____, to whom I was then married, helped in the field work, and a number of the observations in the book are hers.

These are excellent books, and they have taught me a great deal, but then so have the prefaces to them.

If this puts liberated men at a competitive disadvantage, needless to say it does the same to liberated women. It is a familiar joke in women's circles to say, "What I really need is a wife." Young women in graduate school today are, according to the 1969 Carnegie survey, much more likely (63 percent) to have husbands in academe than are men to have academic wives (14 percent). Typed page for typed page, proofread line for proofread line, soothing hour for soothing hour, I suspect that, all else being equal, a traditional male, minus a modern woman, is more likely than anyone else to end up a branch manager.

This total situation is often perceived as a "woman's problem," her role conflict, as if that conflict were detachable from the career system itself. It is her problem to choose between a few prepackaged options: being a housewife, or professor, or trying to piece together a collage of wife, mother, and *traditional* career. The option we do not hear about, one that would make it a man's problem or a university problem as well, is parenthood with a radically new sort of career. Affirmative action plans aren't talking about this.

Given the academic career as it is now, women can only improvise one or another practical solution for fitting their families to their careers. Many professional women of my generation either waited to have children until two years into their first "real" job or had them before beginning graduate school. One had her children in-between and resolved the dual pressures by using her children as data for her books. Those who waited until they were in their late twenties or early thirties often did so precisely to avoid premature discrimination, only to discover that the real pressure point lay not behind but slightly ahead. Nearly half the women who remain in academic life solve the problem by not marrying or not rearing children at all. In a 1962 study of 21,650 men and 2,234 women scientists and engineers, women were six times more likely than men never to marry. Those women who married were less likely than their male colleagues to raise a family: 36 percent of women and 11 percent of men had no children. Those women who did have children had fewer: the families of women scientists and engineers were, compared with those of their male counterparts, one child smaller (David, 1973). Among graduate students, the proportion who consider dropping out increases for women with each new child born, but remains the same for men.[10] Another study of women who received their doctorates between 1958 and 1963 in a number of fields found that only 50 percent of the women had married by 1967. Among the men, 95 percent were married (Simon et al., 1967).

Half of the women and nearly all of the men married; it's a painful little statistic, and I say that without being derogatory to single women. It is one thing for a woman to freely *decide*

[10] According to Carnegie data, 57 percent of men with no children, 58 percent with one, 58 percent with two, and 59 percent with three considered quitting for good in the last year. For women, it was 42 percent with no children, 48 percent for one, 42 percent for two, and 57 percent for three. Three seems to be a crucial number. Among graduate students nationally between 1958 and 1963, 44 percent of men and 55 percent of women actually did drop out, but 49 percent of men with children and 74 percent of women with children did so (Sells, forthcoming doctoral dissertation).

Simon et al. (1967) found that married women without children were slightly less likely to have published a book than were married women with children. Age was not considered, and of course it might account for this otherwise unexpected finding. Forty percent of unmarried, 47 percent of married, and 37 percent of married mothers were assistant professors; 28 percent, 16 percent, 15 percent were associates; and 18 percent, 8 percent, and 8 percent were full professors (Simon et al., 1967). Fifty-eight percent of unmarried women, 33 percent of married, and 28 percent of married women with children (among those earning their degrees in 1958–59) had tenure. Another study comparing men and women showed that 20 years after getting their degrees, 90 percent of the men, 53 percent of the single women, and 41 percent of the married women had reached a full professorship (Rossi, 1970).

against marriage or children as issues on their own merits. But it is quite another matter to be forced into the choice because the career system is shaped for and by the man with a family who is family-free.[11]

SITUATION AND CONSCIOUS-NESS It is for a minority of academic women with children that the contradictions exist in their full glory. My own solution may be uncommon, but not the general contours of my dilemma. When I first decided to have a child at the age of 31, my thoughts turned to the practical arrangements whereby I could continue to teach, something that means a great deal to me. Several arrangements were possible, but my experiment was a preindustrial one—to introduce the family back into the university, to take the baby with me for office hours on the fourth floor of Barrows Hall. From two to eight months, he was, for the most part, the perfect guest. I made him a little cardboard box with blankets where he napped (which he did most of the time), and I brought along an infant seat from which he kept an eye on key chains, colored notebooks, earrings, and glasses. Sometimes waiting students took him out into the hall and passed him around. He became a conversation piece with shy students, and some returned to see him rather than me. I put up a fictitious name on the appointment list every four hours and fed him alone or while on the telephone.

The baby's presence proved to be a Rorschach test, for people reacted very differently. Older men, undergraduate women, and a few younger men seemed to like him and the idea of his being there. In the next office there was a distinguished professor of 74; it was our joke that he would stop by when he heard the baby crying and say, shaking his head, "Beating the baby again, eh?" Publishers and book salesmen in trim suits and exquisite sideburns were generally shocked. Graduate student women would often inquire about him tentatively, and a few feminists were put

---

[11] A woman's college that has administered questionnaires each year since 1964 to entering freshmen found that 65 percent of the class of 1964 wanted to be a housewife with one or more children. In the following years, the percentage dropped steadily: 65, 61, 60, 53, 52, 46, and 31. The proportion who wanted career and marriage with children doubled, from 20 to 40 percent. The difference between Stanford women surveyed in 1965 and in 1972 is even more dramatic: in all, only 18 percent mentioned the role of wife and mother as part of their plans for the next five years (see Carnegie Commission, 1973).

off, perhaps because babies are out of fashion these days, perhaps because his presence seemed "unprofessional."

One incident brought into focus my identity and the university's bizarre power to maintain relationships in the face of change. It happened about a year ago. A male graduate student had come early for his appointment. The baby had slept longer than usual and got hungry later than I had scheduled by Barrows Hall time. I invited the student in. Since we had never met before, he introduced himself with extreme deference. He seemed acquainted with my work and tastes in the field, and as I am often tempted to do, I responded to that deference by behaving more formally than I otherwise might. He began tentatively to elaborate his interests in sociology and to broach the subject of asking me to serve on his orals committee. He had the onerous task of explaining to me that he was a clever student, a trustworthy and obedient student, but that academic fields were not organized as he wanted to study them; and of asking me, without knowing what I thought, whether he could study Marx under the rubric of the sociology of work.

In the course of this lengthy explanation, the baby began to cry. I gave him a pacifier and continued to listen all the more intently. The student went on. The baby spat out the pacifier and began to wail. Finally, trying to be casual, I began to feed him. He wailed now the strongest, most rebellious wail I had ever heard from this small armful of person.

The student uncrossed one leg and crossed the other and held a polite smile, coughing a bit as he waited for this little crisis to pass. I excused myself, and got up to walk back and forth with the baby to calm him down. "I've never done this before. It's just an experiment," I remember saying.

"I have two children of my own," he replied. "Only they're not in Berkeley. We're divorced and I miss them a lot." We exchanged a human glance of mutual support, talked of our families more, and soon the baby calmed down.

A month later when John had signed up for a second appointment, he entered the office, sat down formally. "As we were discussing last time, Professor Hochschild. . . ." Nothing further was said about the prior occasion, but more astonishing to me, nothing had changed. I was still Professor Hochschild and he was still John. Something about power lived on regardless.

In retrospect, I felt a little like one of the characters in *Dr.*

Dolittle and the Pirates, the pushme-pullyu, a horse with two heads that see and say different things. The pushme head was relieved that motherhood had not reduced me as a professional. But the pullyu wondered what the pervasive power differences were doing there in the first place. And why weren't children in offices occasionally part of the "normal" scene?

At the same time I also felt envious of the smooth choiceless-ness of my male colleagues who did not bring their children to Barrows Hall. I sometimes feel this keenly when I meet a male colleague jogging on the track (it's a popular academic sport because it takes little time) and then meet his wife taking their child to the YMCA kinder-gym program. I feel it too when I see wives drive up to the building in the evening, in the station wagon, elbow on the window, two children in the back, waiting for a man briskly walking down the steps, briefcase in hand. It seems a particularly pleasant moment in the day for them. It reminds me of those Friday evenings, always a great treat, when my older brother and I would pack into the back of our old Hudson, and my mother with a picnic basket would drive up from the suburbs to Washington, D.C., at five o'clock to meet my father, walking briskly down the steps of the State Department, briefcase in hand. We picnicked at the Cherry Basin surrounding the Jefferson Memorial, my parents sharing their day, and in that end-of-the-week mood, we came home.

Whenever I see similar scenes, something inside rips in half, for I am neither and both the brisk-stepping carrier of a briefcase and the mother with a packed picnic lunch. The university is designed for such men, and their homes for such women. It looks easier for them and part of me envies them for it. Beneath the envy lies a sense of my competitive disadvantage vis-à-vis the men to whom I am compared and to whom I compare myself. Also beneath it, I am aware of the bizarreness of my experiment with the infant box, and paradoxically aware too that I am envious of a life I would not really like to live.

The invisible half of this scene is, of course, the woman in the station wagon. She has "solved" the problem in one of the other possible ways. But if both her way and my way of solving this "problem" seem to lead to strains, it may be that the problem is not only ours. It may be the inevitable result of a public system arranged not for women with families but for family-free men.

THE WHOLE
OF THE
PROBLEM:
THE PARTS
OF THE
SOLUTION

The problem for American women today is not so much going to work, since over 40 percent of women of working age are in the labor force already and nine out of ten women work some time in their lives. The problem is now one of moving *up,* and that means moving into careers. More fundamentally, the problem for women in academic or other sorts of careers is to alter the link between family and career, and more generally, between private and public life. Several alternatives seem both possible and just. First, women might adopt a relation to home and family indistinguishable from that of their male competitors. Women could marry househusbands if they can find them, or hire a substitute wife-mother in their absence. Academic women could thereby establish a two-roled life for another person (a husband), or divide such roles between husband and housekeeper. If the housekeeper were well paid and unionized, perhaps we could still talk about justice; otherwise I think not. But neither a housekeeper nor a child-care center would solve the problem completely, since tending the sick, caring for the old, writing Christmas cards, and just being there for people in their bad moments—what wives do—still need doing. In my view, even when we have eliminated the needless elaboration of a wife's role, a humanly satisfying life requires that someone do these things.

Second, academic men who want careers might give up marriage or children, just as many academic women have. If the first alternative makes women more like men, this one makes men more like academic women, in extending to them the familiar two-box choice of family or career. This would be more just, but I doubt it would be popular among men.

One can understand women who opt for the first alternative, given the absence of other choices. Insofar as it involves a reverse family imperialism, however, I do not see why it is any better than the original male one. Because I value at least the option of family life, I cannot endorse the second solution either. Since neither appeals to me as a long-range solution, I am led to a third alternative: the possibility of an egalitarian marriage with a radically different career to go with it. This means creating a different system in which to work at this different career, a system that would make egalitarian marriage *normal.*

The university makes virtually no adjustments to the family, but the traditional family makes quite a few to the university. And it is not so much the brisk-stepping man with the briefcase as it is his wife with the picnic basket who makes the adjustments for "the family's sake" (somehow amorphously connected to his career.) I think the reason for this is that it is easier to change families than universities. But the contradictions of changing families without changing careers leads to either migraine headaches or hearty, rebellious thoughts.

Any vision of changing something as apparently implacable as the career system may seem at first ludicrous or utopian. But as Karl Mannheim (1936) once pointed out, all movements for social change need a utopia, built of parts borrowed from different or theoretical societies. This need not be a utopia for dreaming that remains separate from waking life, but a utopia that, like reading a good book, shows us where and how far we have to go, a vision that makes sense of frustration by analyzing its source. In the 1970s, when utopias already seem quaint, when public visions seem a large shadow over many small private aims, when jobs are scarce and competition magnified, now in the 1970s more than ever we need a guiding vision.

For a start, all departments of 20 full-time men could expand to departments of 40 part-time men and women. This would offer a solution to our present dilemma of trying to meet the goals of affirmative action within a "steady state" (or declining) economy. It would mean more jobs for women and men. It would democratize and thus eliminate competitive disadvantages and offer an opportunity to some of those women in the station wagon. In many fields, research would leap ahead if two people rather than one worked on problems. Teaching would certainly not be hurt by the arrangement and might benefit from the additional energies.

While administrative arrangements would be manageable, I can imagine queries about efficiency. Is it economical to train 40 Ph.D's to work part-time when 20 could do the same amount of work? And what of those who simply do not want part-time work? One can point to the new glut of Ph.D.'s and argue that if those currently teaching in universities were to divide and share their jobs, many more might gain the chance to work. The effect would not eliminate but reduce competition for university jobs.

Part-time work is very often more like three-fourths-time

work, for one teaches students rather than classes. If a graduate student moves to Ecuador and sends me his paper, I read it. If a former student comes around to the house, I talk to her. If there is a meeting, I don't leave halfway through the hour. Part-time often turns out to be a release in quantity to improve quality.

But that raises the financial issue. The sorry fact is that, for financial reasons, most men and some women do not want half-time work. A male professor may work long hours when his children are young and there are doctor bills, and again when they are in college and there are tuition bills. But two part-time workers earn two part-time salaries, and there are social disadvantages to the one overworked–one underworked family pattern.

Hearsay has it that a group of MIT male assistant professors, who had worked late evenings because they were in competition with each other for advancement while their wives took care of the children, made a pact to cut down their hours and spend more time with their young children. Maybe many private pacts could lead to a larger public one, but only when those who set the standards are part of it.

While one may debate the virtues or defects of competition, it is an aspect of university life that we need not take for granted, that can be, and I think should be, modified. Some elements of my own utopia are borrowed from the Cuban experiment, since it bears on the issue of competition. The Cuban revolution made its share of mistakes, and not all of its successes are applicable to a rich industrial country. But the basic lesson to be learned from Cuba is that competition can be modified not only by splitting jobs (which it did not try to do), but by creating jobs to fit social needs. This may seem a bit far afield in an essay on universities, but my analysis brings me to it. For in my view, we cannot change the role of women in universities without changing the career system based on competition, and we can't change that competitive structure without also altering the economy, the larger fit of supply and demand of workers. We need thus to explore the experiments in altering that.

I visited the University of Havana in the summer of 1967 and joined some students and faculty who were working together doing "productive labor" (they don't think this phrase is redundant), planting coffee plants in the belt surrounding Havana. As we moved along the rows, people talked about the university before the revolution. It sounded in some ways like a more intense version of Berkeley in both the 1960s and 1970s.

The competition was so fierce for the few professional jobs in the cities that rich students bought grades. (That is only one step removed from the profitable cynicism of the term paper industries, like "Quality Bullshit" in Berkeley, where a student can buy a custom-written paper from some unemployed graduate students.)

At the same time, Cuban students hung around the university cafes dropping out and back in again, wondering who they were. Before 1958 there were some 3,000 students at the University of Havana trying to enter the diplomatic service, while there was only a handful of electrical engineers in the whole country. The revolution put the university in touch with economic realities, and it changed those economic realities by inventing jobs where there was a social need for them. Since the revolution, the task has not been to restrict admission, but to supply the tremendous need for doctors, dentists, teachers, and architects as clients of the poor, paid by the government. The revolution simply recognized and legitimated a need that had always been there.

Corresponding to the supply of graduates American universities turn out each year, there is, I believe, a "social need." There is, for example, a great need for teachers in crowded classrooms, and yet we speak of the teacher "surplus." Despite the AMA, and the fierce competition to enter medical school, we need doctors, especially in ghettos and in prisons. We need quality day care, community organizers, traveling artists. Yet there are, we say, "too many people" and "not enough jobs." If social need coincided with social demand for skills, if market value were coextensive with use value, we could at least in some fields eliminate *needless* competition generated outside the university, which affects what goes on inside as well. I personally do not think "education for leisure" is the answer, for it ignores all the social ills that persist even in a rich industrial country, not to mention those outside it. If we redefine what a social need is, and design jobs to meet social needs, we also reduce the exaggerated competition we see in universities, a competition that inevitably moves women out. If the division of jobs alleviates competition among academics, the creation of jobs can alleviate competition among would-be workers, including, of course, professors.[12]

There is another lesson to be learned from Cuba, too. Insofar as American career women become like career men, they become oriented toward success and competition. Just as manhood has traditionally been measured by success, so now academic womanhood is defined that way. But manhood, for the middle-class American academic man, is based *more* on "doing well" than on "doing good." Manhood in professional circles is linked to an orientation toward "success," which is kept scarce and made to seem valuable. Men are socialized to competition because they are socialized to scarcity. It is as if sexual identity, at least in the middle class, were not freely given by nature, but conserved only for those who earn it. Manhood at birth seems to be taken from men, only for them to re-win it. The bookish boy is defined as girlish and then, with a turnabout, earns his manhood as a creative scholar in the university. To fail to "do well" at this is to be robbed in degrees of manhood.

I think there is a human propensity to achieve competence, what Thorstein Veblen (1914) called simply an "instinct for workmanship," but it comes to have a secondary meaning for *manhood*. The competition that takes the form of secrecy attached to new ideas before they are in final draft for the publisher, the vita talk, the 60-hour work weeks, the station wagon wife, all are related to this secondary meaning of work, this second layer of value associated with success and manhood. It is this second meaning that women feel they must analogously adopt and compete with.

Yet the reputation so won is often totally detached from social usefulness or moral purpose. For such men, *morality* has become a *luxury*. Women who learn to aspire to this deficiency lose what was valuable from our first training—a training not only to be invisible, but, in a larger sense, to "do good" rather than simply to "do well." Insofar as women, like other marginal groups,

[12] How a nation or university "legislates" that supply meets demand for jobs without becoming authoritarian raises not simply an administrative but a serious political issue to which I have no easy answer. Here I only mean to show that dividing up old jobs and creating new ones is a possible way of alleviating competition that underlies the career system.

overconform in the attempt to gain acceptance, we find ourselves even more oriented toward success, and less toward morality, than some men.

The Cuban revolution seems to me to have solved at least this dilemma, simply by trying structurally to equate "doing well" with "doing good," achievement with moral purpose. The assimilation of Cuban women entering a male-dominated economy does not seem to mean the eclipse of morality. Cuban women have not escaped the doll's house to enter a career of "bourgeois individualism"; they have, despite other problems, escaped that as well.

CONCLUSION To talk as I have about the evils of the system as they affect a handful of academic women is a little like talking about the problems of the suburb while there are people trying to escape the ghetto. But there are problems both with trying to find a meaningful career and with having one on the system's terms. The two problems are more than distantly related. Both finding an academic job and remaining humane once you have had one for a while are problems that lead ultimately to the assumptions about families that lie behind careers. At present, women are either slowly eliminated from academic life or else forced imperceptibly to acquire the moral and psychic disabilities from which male academics have had to suffer.

If we are to bring more women into the university at every level, we shall have to do something more extreme than most affirmative action plans have imagined: change the present entente between the university and its service agency, the family. If we change this, we also introduce into academe some of the values formerly the separate specialty of women. We leaven the ethos of "making it" with another ethos of caretaking and cooperation, leaven the *gesellschaft* with the values of *gemeinschaft*. It is, after all, not simply women but some feminine values that have been discriminated against. It is not simply that we lack role models who happen to be women, but that we lack exemplars of this alternative ethos.

What I am trying to say is that social justice, giving women a fair break, is a goal that speaks for itself, and a goal that calls for men doing their fair share in private life and for women getting their fair chance in public life. But there are two ways of creating this social justice. One involves fitting into the meritocracy as it is; the other aims to change it. Insofar as we merely extend "bourgeois individualism" to women, ask for "a room of one's own," a reputation, sparring with the others, we fit in nicely with the normal distortion of the importance of success versus moral purpose, the experience of time, or quality of talk that men experience.

The very first step is to reconsider what parts in the cultural recipe of our first socialization to nurturance and caring are worth salvaging in ourselves, and the second step is to consider how to extend and institutionalize them in our place of work. The second way of creating social justice less often speaks up for itself: it is to democratize and reward that cooperative, caretaking, morally concerned, not-always-lived-up-to womanly virtue of the past. We need *that* in careers, that among our full professors of either sex. My utopian university is not a Tolstoyan peasant family, but it is also not vita talking to vita. It requires a move in the balance between competition and cooperation, doing well and doing good, taking time to teach a child to swim and taking time to vote in a department meeting. When we have made that change, surely it will show in book prefaces and office talk.

REFERENCES

Astin, Helen: *The Woman Doctorate in America,* Russell Sage Foundation, New York, 1969.

Bernard, Jessie: *Academic Women,* World Publishing Company, New York, 1966.

Carnegie Commission on Higher Education: *Opportunities for Women in Higher Education,* McGraw-Hill Book Company, New York, 1973.

David, Deborah: "Marriage and Fertility Patterns of Scientists and Engineers: A Comparison of Males and Females," paper delivered at the American Sociological Association Convention, New York, September 1973.

Ervin-Tripp, Susan M.: "Report of the Committee on the Status of Women," University of California, Berkeley, May 21, 1973.

Feldman, Saul: *Escape from the Doll's House: Women in Graduate and Professional School Education,* McGraw-Hill Book Company, New York, 1974.

Graham, Patricia A.: "Women in Academe," in Athena Theodore (ed.), *The Professional Woman,* Schenkman Publishing Co., Inc., Cambridge, Mass., 1971, pp. 720–740.

Kerr, Clark: *The Uses of the University,* Harvard University Press, Cambridge, Mass., 1963.

Kriegel, Leonard: *Working Through,* Saturday Review Press, New York, 1972.

Lee, Dorothy: *Freedom and Culture,* Prentice-Hall, Englewood Cliffs, N.J., 1965.

Lehman, H.: *Age and Achievement,* Princeton University Press, Princeton, N.J., 1953.

Lehman, H.: "More About Age and Achievement," *The Gerontologist,* vol. 2, no. 3, 1962.

Lehman, H.: "The Production of Masterworks Prior to Age Thirty," *The Gerontologist,* vol. 5, no. 1, pp. 24–29, 1965.

Lofting, Hugh: *Dr. Dolittle and the Pirates,* Beginner Books, a division of Random House, Inc., New York, 1968.

Mannheim, Karl: *Ideology and Utopia, an Introduction to the Sociology of Knowledge,* L. Wirth and E. Shils (trans.), Harcourt, Brace, London, 1936.

Mitchell, Susan: *Women and the Doctorate,* U.S. Department of Health, Education and Welfare, Office of Education, Bureau of Research, Washington, D.C., 1968.

Papanek, Hanna: "Men, Women, and Work: Reflections on the Two-Person Career," in Joan Huber (ed.), *Changing Women in a Changing Society,* The University of Chicago Press, Chicago, 1973.

Rossi, Alice S.: "Status of Women in Graduate Departments of Sociology," *The American Sociologist,* vol. 5, pp. 1–12, February 1970.

Rossi, Alice S., and **Ann Calderwood** (eds.): *Academic Women on the Move,* Russell Sage Foundation, New York, 1973.

Sells, Lucy: Forthcoming doctoral dissertation, University of California, Berkeley.

Simon, Rita J., Shirley M. Clark, and **Kathleen Galway:** "The Woman Ph.D.: A Recent Profile," *Social Problems,* vol. 15, pp. 221–236, 1967.

Veblen, Thorstein: *The Instinct of Workmanship and the State of the Industrial Arts,* Viking Press, New York, 1914.

3. A View from the Law School

by Aleta Wallach*

The university is a transmitter of social values and class interests hostile to women. It oppresses women because it negates women's history and culture by ignoring or distorting them. Law is the archetypal enforcer of these social values and class interests hostile to women transmitted by the university. It follows, then, that legal education is doubly oppressive to women, because it is the study of law—the maintenance institution—which sanctions and authorizes, at times mandates, antifeminist social values and class interests.

I shall begin by describing the relation between legal education and law itself and their relation to our society. Then I shall consider the role of women relative to all three of these institutions. While there are obvious parallels in the relationship between women and other professional schools and professions (and I shall allude to medicine on occasion), I choose to focus on the legal education of women not only because that is what I know experientially, but mainly because the subject matter of legal education, unlike other professional education, is the formulation and enforcement of differential statuses for certain classes of persons. That law has effectively conferred upon women, who as a class constitute over half of United States' population, an inferior status is a curious phenomenon indeed. Even more curious, however, is that this phenomenon is not a pervasive subject in legal education and, until recently, has been ignored altogether. Where the subject of women's status is now noted in legal education, it is regarded as second-class and nonessential.

* I want here to express my abiding love and gratitude to Donald Kalish, who has given to me and to all my writings part of his life.

RULE OF MEN, NOT RULE OF LAW

My first awareness of the real world came when I entered law school. I was 23. Until that time I had lived primarily in the world of my mind, as an artist, poet, and dreamer. Because my consciousness was entirely derived from my own private illusion of absolute freedom, I was unaware of any limitations on my will, and unaware of any differences of class or privilege between me and men. Consequently I had no feminist consciousness, no identification of myself *qua* woman. I was, so I thought, a "person," and as a creative and imaginative one, the entire universe in all its glorious variety was my clay.

It was altogether predictable, then, that the first thing I discovered, once in law school, was that the real world was indeed a different place. I saw the society in which I lived defined and structured in terms of its most primary institution—law.[1] This highly complex structure creates and controls hierarchical relationships among persons by granting or imposing power, privilege, right, duty, liability, and immunity, as the case may be, among specific persons or classes of persons. Status, therefore, is the subject matter of law. I came to see law as the source of all power, indeed as power itself, conferring or withholding status as it does.

In a law school where all faculty members but one were male, where our casebooks as well as the judicial opinions contained therein were written by men, and where the students, future lawyers, were primarily males, this view of law was not taught to us directly in our standard torts, contracts, property, or criminal law courses. Rather I learned it indirectly by piecing together parts of separate substantive areas to create an overview. It occurred to me that over 90 percent of United States law pertains to property and that, since both statutes and cases promote the interests of the propertied class against the nonpropertied class, law is capitalism's main support. It is true that in recent times law has begun to create rights for the nonpropertied class as against the propertied class, substituting for this latter's right a duty. Such change is apparent in the legal relationships of landlord and tenant, consumer and manufacturer. But changes in law occur at

[1] Although it can be argued that the institution of family or education or even economy (capitalism) is the primary institution of society, I believe that these institutions are secondary to law because it is law that provides the superstructure in which they exist and authorizes their particular forms.

a snail's pace, and decades or centuries[2] are required before emergent doctrines are accepted. For law, relying as it does on precedent and tradition, is essentially a backward-looking rather than forward-looking institution. Thus, the law, especially judicial interpretation, generally is not an instrument for social change. (That function is reserved to representative bodies, the legislatures.) Law functions, then, to maintain the status quo.[3]

Although the law school curriculum never explicitly presented the full picture, it was obvious enough that women are among the classes of persons disfavored by law. Women's legal heritage is that of nonpersons, of beings whose existences are relational to fathers, husbands, and children. Even the Supreme Court applies a lower standard of judicial review to classifications based upon sex than it does to classifications based upon race or alienage.[4] A few examples will illustrate how law creates women's inferior status by conferring powers, rights, privileges, duties, liabilities, and immunities upon them vis-à-vis men. In New Jersey

[2] Consider, for example, the century of women's struggle required to achieve franchise with the adoption in 1920 of the Nineteenth Amendment to the United States Constitution. The abortion reform and repeal movements pressed their arguments in courts of law for decades before antiabortion statutes were declared unconstitutional by the Supreme Court in the companion cases *Roe v. Wade* (1973) and *Doe v. Bolton* (1973).

[3] The astute if paternalistic observer of the American scene, Alexis de Tocqueville, in the early 1830s accounted for this fundamental characteristic of the United States legal system: "In America there are no nobles or literary men, and the people are apt to mistrust the wealthy; lawyers consequently form the highest political class and the most cultivated portion of society. They have therefore nothing to gain by innovation, which adds a conservative interest to their natural taste for public order. If I were asked where I place the American aristocracy, I should reply without hesitation that it is not among the rich, who are united by no common tie, but that it occupies the judicial bench and bar.

"The more we reflect upon all that occurs in the United States, the more we shall be persuaded that the lawyers, as a body, form the most powerful, if not the only, counterpoise to the democratic element. In that country we easily perceive how the legal profession is qualified by its attributes, and even by its faults, to neutralize the vices inherent in popular government. When the American people are intoxicated by passion or carried away by the impetuosity of their ideas, they are checked and stopped by the almost invisible influence of their legal counselors. These secretly oppose their aristocratic propensities to the nation's democratic instincts, their superstitious attachment to what is old, to its love of novelty, their narrow views to its immense designs, and their habitual procrastination to its ardent impatience" (Tocqueville, 1956, pp. 288–289).

[4] Compare *Reed v. Reed* (1972) and *Frontiero v. Richardson* (1973) with *Korematsu v. United States* (1944) (race) and *Graham v. Richardson* (1971) (alienage).

a husband has the *power* to determine his wife's domicile,[5] and in California, Civil Code section 5101 declares the husband to be the head of the family and gives him the *right* to choose the place and mode of living and imposes upon the wife the corresponding *duty* to conform thereto. California Probate Code sections 202 and 203 give a husband an automatic *right* to his intestate wife's half of the community property, but upon a husband's death his wife has *no right* to receive even her own half of the community property until the entire community property goes through probate. California Penal Code section 26 *immunizes* from responsibility a married woman who commits a misdemeanor under the threat or command of her husband by denying to her legal capacity to commit such an offense. A husband has the *privilege* of raping his wife since, by definition under California Penal Code section 261, rape cannot be committed by a woman's own husband. Finally, in Texas a husband has the *right* to use deadly force upon another who was at the time of the homicide in the act of intercourse with his wife, but a wife is *liable* to criminal punishment for killing another in the act of intercourse with her husband.[6]

These illustrations should be sufficient to indicate that in law women are pawns in a men's game, a very serious game because the stakes are so high—personal life, liberty, happiness, and perhaps even survival of the human species. In a game played by both women and men but for which men have made all the rules, it is unlikely that any woman would win. In law, women were never intended to "win" if "winning" means participating in the formulation (legislating) and application (judging) of a body of rules that controls conduct and status through the imposition of benefits and detriments upon persons and classes of persons. The intentional exclusion of women from participation in any aspect of law is evident in the fact that women were denied the right to vote, thus ensuring that men, the only voters, could electorally constitute themselves as the lawmakers—the legislators. We have seen what rules of law they have made. In addition men took it upon themselves to judicially declare, as a rule of law, that women could not be lawyers—the practitioners of law, and eventually the judges of law. The opinion of the

---

[5] *In re Paullin* (1921).

[6] Texas Penal Code art. 1220 (Vernon's 1961); *Reed v. State* (1933).

Supreme Court itself rested on the ground that the practice of law is not a right protected by the federal Constitution. But Mr. Justice Bradley, concurring in *Bradwell v. Illinois* (1872), the United States Supreme Court case holding that women could constitutionally be denied a license to practice law, went on to declare that:

Man is, or should be, woman's protector and defender. The natural and proper timidity and delicacy which belongs to the female sex evidently unfits it for many of the occupations of civil life. The constitution of the family organization, which is founded in the divine ordinance, as well as in the nature of things, indicates the domestic sphere as that which properly belongs to the domain and functions of womanhood. The harmony, not to say identity, of interests and views which belong, or should belong, to the family institution is repugnant to the idea of a woman adopting a distinct and independent career from that of her husband. . . . The paramount destiny and mission of woman are to fulfill the noble and benign offices of wife and mother. This is the law of the Creator. And the rules of civil society must be adopted to the general constitution of things, and cannot be based upon exceptional cases (*Bradwell v. Illinois*, 1872, pp. 141–142).[7]

It is important to realize exactly what teamwork men played here. The Illinois Legislature, elected exclusively by men, had passed a law vesting in the State Supreme Court the *power* of granting licenses to practice law. Accordingly, Myra Bradwell applied to the judges of the Illinois Supreme Court for a license to practice law. She accompanied her petition with the usual certificate from an inferior court that she possessed good character and that upon due examination she had also been found to possess the requisite qualifications. Her first application to the Illinois Supreme Court was refused, and the court stated as a sufficient reason that, according to Illinois decisional law, Myra Bradwell "as a married woman would be bound neither by her express contracts nor by those implied contracts which it is the policy of the law to create between attorney and client" (quoted in *Bradwell v. Illinois*, 1872, p. 131). Myra Bradwell pressed further her right to admission to the state bar, and the court thereupon issued a written opinion [*In re Bradwell*, 1869, pp. 535, 539] which said, *inter alia*:

[7] Although *Bradwell* has not been overruled by the United States Supreme Court, no state today categorically denies women license to practice law.

That God designed the sexes to occupy different spheres of action, and that it belonged to men to make, apply, and execute the laws, was regarded as an almost axiomatic truth. . . .

In view of these facts, we are certainly warranted in saying, that when the legislature gave to this court the power of granting licenses to practice law, it was with not the slightest expectation that this *privilege* would be extended equally to men and women [Emphasis added].

Her application thus having been denied by the state supreme court, Bradwell appealed to the United States Supreme Court, which affirmed the denial.

The Illinois Legislature, elected by men, granted *power* to judges on the Illinois Supreme Court, who were men, to determine if women could practice law in that state. The Legislature threw the ball to an inferior court that smoothly passed it to the court of last resort without fumble or tackle. It is to be noted that the opinions of both the state and federal Supreme Courts used self-appointed power to make their decision. In order to create a rule of law that would serve their own interests as men, to maintain women in a position of servitude within the family to service their lives, and thus to preserve their privilege and freedom, both courts invoked a law higher than civil law to justify this rule. They relied on divine and natural law. In so doing, they went outside of the agreed-upon rules of the game—that is, the application of statutes, precedential decisions, and policy of their *own* making—and instead invoked an authority higher than themselves to justify what cannot be viewed as anything other than a rule of men, meaning those particular men who exercised their power oppressively. And it should not be forgotten that since the business of law schools is to service the legal community by producing lawyers, and inasmuch as law schools—being but one cog, the preparatory one, in the wheel of law—respond to the needs of the legal community and of society itself, *Bradwell* could only be a strong incentive to refuse women admission to law school. Since the practice of law was not a privilege extended to women, it would indeed be a waste of academic resources to prepare women lawyers instead of men.

The invocation of divine and natural law as justifications for the decision in *Bradwell* was merely a covert way for individual men to substitute their self-serving interests and prejudices for a rule of law and yet give the appearance of deciding the case according to a rule of law: divine and natural law are not part of the civil domain that we understand to be applicable rules of law. Moreover, this rule of men (meaning individual male persons) that purported to be a rule of law *became* a rule of law in terms of its precedential value for future cases. This is an extremely important observation, because the entire system of Anglo-American law characterizes and justifies itself as based upon the "rule of law" rather than the "rule of men." (It is always pretended, of course, that "men" in this context generically means individuals of both sexes, not just males, but this has not been the case.) Indeed democracy distinguishes itself from monarchy by this basic difference in form. In democracy almost all interactions between human beings are governed by neutral regulations that constitute the rule of law, and at least in principle no individual can affect another individual except within the framework of agreed-upon rules that govern their relationships. In reality, however, many of these regulations were made by men for the benefit of men (meaning males), so that although we have perhaps evolved from a rule of men (meaning individual persons) into a rule of law in a formal sense, as far as women are concerned I contend that we still live under a rule of men, that is, the class of males. In democracy, rule of law is created by men and favors men: thus it could be said that males now rule much as individual persons did under monarchy. There is a subtle difference though. They no longer rule by arbitrary fiat, as in monarchy, but rather by a set of rules that enables them to say that government is a rule of law, not men. Thus although particular male individuals can now no longer make arbitrary rules in particular cases, the class of men has made arbitrary self-serving rules and passes them off as the rules of law by which principled decisions are made.

It was not easy to discover the reality that lurked behind those revered words, "rule of law not rule of men," that embodied a precept of neutrality and fairness very basic to legal theory and education. I eventually unearthed their hidden meaning, although no course except legal philosophy had as its actual subject matter the rule of law. By the time I enrolled in legal philosophy, I was already doubtful of the actual existence of the rule of law with respect to women, having observed in class after class that doctrinal exceptions were continually made that effectively excluded women from its purview.

Legal philosophy is an elective course for second- and third-year students and its usual enrollment is small. The course examines selected topics concerning the nature of law and the relationship of law to morals, including the relationship between the process of decision making and the process of justification. During our seemingly endless abstract discussions I came to reject the possibility, let alone reality, of rule of law in our society. Each time the professor talked about the rule of law as the finding and application of neutral principles on a case-by-case basis, he and I engaged in extended and sometimes angry dialogue, neither succeeding in convincing the other of his and her respective positions. As far as I could see then, the concept of neutral, doctrinal decision making was just that—a concept. The doctrines themselves are, at this point, too contaminated with the arbitrary, oppressive self-interest of men to be more than the rule of men, meaning males collectively.

One further example may clarify the way men have manipulated law in order to oppress women and why I think the rule of men (meaning not persons individually but males collectively) characterizes our present legal system.

In 1905 the United States Supreme Court in *Lochner v. New York* (198 U.S. 45) invalidated a New York statute that provided that no worker, male or female, could be required or permitted to work in a bakery more than 60 hours in a week or 10 hours in a day. Three years later that same Court, in *Muller v. Oregon* (208 U.S. 412), upheld an Oregon statute substantially similar to the New York statute except that it applied to female workers only. The Supreme Court in *Muller* approved its earlier decision in *Lochner* on the grounds that the law was not, "as to men, a legitimate exercise of police power of the state, but an unreasonable, unnecessary, and arbitrary interference with the right and liberty of the individual to contract in relation to his labor, and as such was in conflict with, and void under the Federal Constitution" (*Muller v. Oregon*, 1908, p. 419). Mr. Justice Brewer, writing for the Court, took "judicial cognizance of all matters of general knowledge" (ibid., pp. 421–423):

That woman's physical structure and the performance of maternal functions place her at a disadvantage in the struggle for subsistence is obvious. This is especially true when the burdens of motherhood are upon her. Even when they are not, by abundant testimony of the medical *fraternity* continuance for a long time on her feet at work, repeating this from day to day, tends to injurious effects upon the body, and as healthy mothers are essential to vigorous offspring, the physical well being of woman becomes an object of public interest and care in order to preserve the strength and vigor of the race.

Still again, history discloses the fact that woman has always been dependent upon man. He established his control at the outset by his superior physical strength, and this control in various forms, with diminishing intensity, has continued to the present. As minors, though not to the same extent, she has been looked upon in the courts as needing especial care that her rights may be preserved. Education was long denied her, and while now the doors of the school room are opened and her opportunities for acquiring knowledge are great, yet even with that and the consequent increase of capacity for business affairs it is still true that in the struggle for subsistence she is not an equal competitor with her brother. Though limitations upon personal and contractual rights may be removed by legislation, there is that in her disposition and habits of life which will operate against a full assertion of those rights. She will still be where some legislation to protect her seems necessary to secure a real equality of right. Doubtless there are individual exceptions, and there are many respects in which she has an advantage over him: but looking at it from the viewpoint of the effort to maintain an independent position in life, she is not upon an equality. Differentiated by these matters from the other sex, she is properly placed in a class by herself, and legislation designed for her protection may be sustained, even when like legislation is not necessary for men and could not be sustained. It is impossible to close one's eyes to the fact that she still looks to her brother and depends upon him. Even though all restrictions on political, personal and contractual rights were taken away, and she stood, so far as statutes are concerned, upon an absolutely equal plane with him, it would still be true that she is so constituted that she will rest upon and look to him for protection: that her physical structure and a proper discharge of her maternal functions—having in view not merely her own health, but the well-being of the race—justify legislation to protect her from the greed as well as the passion of man. The limitations which this statute places upon her contractual powers, upon the right to agree with her employer as to the time she shall labor, are not imposed solely for her benefit, but also largely for the benefit of all. Many words cannot make this plainer. The two sexes differ in structure of body, in the functions to be performed by each, in the amount of physical strength, in the capacity for long-continued labor, particularly when done standing, the influence of vigorous health upon the future well-being of the race, the self-reliance which enables one to assert full rights, and in the capacity to maintain the struggle for subsistence. This difference justifies a difference in legislation and upholds that which is designed to compensate for some of the burdens which rest upon her [Emphasis supplied].

This case established as a matter of law that women are beings whose legal status is relational to others, because it articulated the principle that sex is a valid basis for classification. This principle has, of course, been used to impose restrictions on women and to bestow corresponding benefits upon men.[8] Often the restrictions imposed upon women have been disguised as benefits, like the protective legislation that was fought for and won by exploited working women. Laws that disable women from full participation in the political, business, and economic arenas are often characterized as "protective" and beneficial but upon closer inspection have proved to be cages. By not applying to both females and males, such legislation confers an inferior status upon women and deters their employment because special treatment by employers is required for women under protective legislation.[9]

With law, then, men created a world of power: women were not intended to participate in that world or share that power.[10] Yet despite the exclusion of half of humanity, men undertook through their intricate legal structure of legislation and judicial checks to assign status to all persons: to confer upon women inferior status and upon men preeminent status, and to call it rule of law. By definition, therefore, law—in conception, education,

---

[8] Although some inferior federal courts and some state courts have not followed the rule of *Muller* and have instead invalidated some "protective" legislation, because the United States Supreme Court has never overruled *Muller* it is still valid law.

[9] See *Sail'er Inn, Inc. v. Kirby* (1971, p. 20).

[10] "The notion that men and women stand as equals before the law was not the original understanding. Thomas Jefferson put it this way: 'Were our state a pure democracy there would still be excluded from our deliberations women, who, to prevent deprivation of morals and ambiguity of issues, should not mix promiscuously in gatherings of men.'

"Alexis de Tocqueville, some years later, included this observation among his commentaries on life in the young United States: 'In no country has such constant care been taken as in America to trace two clearly distinct lines of action for the two sexes, and to make them keep pace one with the other, but in two pathways which are always different. American women never manage the outward concerns of the family, or conduct a business, or take a part in political life'" (from Davidson, Ginsburg, & Kay, 1974, p. 2).

and practice—is a male institution. The law school is a feeder institution, producing lawyers to supply the needs of the legal profession and the judiciary. For this reason legal education cannot be realistically appraised apart from the demands of the entities it feeds. Ultimately, of course, the nature of the legal profession and the judiciary is determined by the demands of our society. But one thing is clear. The world of law that I have been describing has not developed with the inclusion of women's values and culture. Thus I found an inherent contradiction in being both a woman and a law student, and now I find an inherent contradiction in being both a woman and a lawyer. Not only are the structure and tools of law not my own, they belong to my oppressor. I think this contradiction will continue as long as the institution of law remains intact. Law, however, can only remain intact as long as it remains insular and women are excluded from it. And since apparently women are now in law to stay, it must be law itself that yields to this tension and changes to accommodate women and women's culture. That this is already beginning to happen is readily apparent by the mass influx of women into law schools and women's vigorous participation in various legal reform movements. The unresolved question is the nature and scope of that transformation.

Before turning to this question, however, I want to review women's historical participation in the Continental, English, and Anglo-American legal systems, for there is more than a little truth to the statement that women entering the study of law today are but retaking that which belongs to them.

WOMEN'S HISTORICAL PARTICIPATION IN LAW

Women in Continental and English law[11]

In 1100 Countess Matilda of Tuscany established the chair of jurisprudence at the University of Bologna, where other women —Laura Bassi, Clotilde Tambroni, and Novella Calderin— studied and received recognition. After they were appointed to important positions in society, they returned to their alma mater to lecture on law. From the eighth to the eleventh century in Spain, women served as judges and jurists and lectured in Cordoba, Granada, and Seville. In the fifteenth century Cassandra Felice received the doctor of laws degree when she was 21

---

[11] The following discussion is derived from Pettus (1900, pp. 325, 326).

years of age. It is thought that she might have been dean or professor of jurisprudence in Padua, since she conferred degrees there. In 1335 Novella D'Andrea was a renowned professor of canon law.

Women participated in law not only in Continental Europe but in England also. Queen Eleanor acted as custodian of the seals, presided in Aula Regia (the queen's hall or palace), which was the chief court of England in early Norman times, and heard causes there. Anne, Countess of Pembroke, was sheriff of Westmoreland. Women of property held hereditary offices in the Court of King's/Queen's Bench, and as high constable, great chamberlain, champion at the coronation, clerk of the crown, regent, and queen.

It is claimed that the origin of English law itself was a set of statutes prepared by one of Britain's early queens. It is said that Alfred the Great adopted the laws of a queen named *Proba,* or the Just, which included trial by jury and the just descent of property among other statutory provisions. Nevertheless, according to fleeting mention in Warren (1911, p. 26), in 1376 Parliament forbade women to practice law or "sue in court by way of maintenance or reward," specifically naming one Alice Ferrars, the unpopular "mistress" of Edward III.

Women in Anglo-American law

In prerevolutionary days, before law became a paid and influential profession and legal training became formalized and institutionalized, women as well as men were attorneys (Lerner, 1971, p. 46). At this time the word *attorney* did not designate a person educated in law who practiced it as an exclusive employment. Rather, early attorneys were traders, factors, land owners, and lay persons who, possessing a talent for writing and argument, brought suits on their own behalf or on behalf of others who employed them to appear and speak in court (Warren, 1911, pp. 4–5).

In this capacity and at this time, in the Maryland Colony, there appeared Margaret Brent, the first American woman attorney. Brent acted as executrix of the estate of Leonard Calvert, first Lord Proprietor and Governor of Maryland, and was regarded by the courts as his attorney. She practiced in all the courts of the colony and appears 124 times in the court records between 1642 and 1650 (Lerner, 1972, p. 32). In addition she was influential in the political affairs of the colony. Brent was the first American woman to insist upon her right to participate in a General Assembly, which in the colonies also constituted the sole courts of law (Warren, 1911, p. 1):

Jan. 21, 1647-8—came Mrs. Margaret Brent in the house for herselfe and voyce also, for that att the last court 3rd Jan. it was ordered that Mrs. Brent was to be looked uppon and received as his Lps. [Lordship's] attorney. The Gov'r denied that the sd. Mrs. Brent should have any vote in the howse. And the sd. Mrs. Brent protested agst all proceedings in this first Assembly unless shee may be pst and have the vote as aforesaid (Warren, 1911, p. 52).

In addition, Margaret Brent owned and managed manorial estates and thus had the right to hold feudal court sessions in which she dispensed justice (Lerner, 1971, p. 17).

In the latter part of the eighteenth century the American legal system became more organized: compulsory apprenticeship coupled with formal examination was increasingly instituted (Stevens, 1971, p. 412). As voluntarily or compulsorily apprenticed lawyers took over litigation, women appear to have disappeared from the court for over a century (Lerner, 1971, p. 46). It is interesting that as women disappeared from participation in law, the legal profession consolidated its power and prestige. Formalized apprenticeship led to the eventual establishment of private law schools, usually outgrowths of the law offices of practitioners who were particularly skilled or popular as teachers.

From an early stage, moreover, the newly organizing legal profession gave preferential treatment to college graduates (Warren, 1911, chap. 9). The importance of this fact is striking when one realizes that at this time there were no women college graduates. It was not until 1833 that the first college, Oberlin, admitted women (Flexner, 1970, p. 29). Furthermore the American college was receptive to introducing the study of law into its curriculum. By the early 1820s colleges began to provide an umbrella under which private law schools could develop. Private law schools affiliated with colleges because they gained prestige thereby, and because for the most part only colleges were empowered to grant degrees. Thus began the American law school as a systematic institution which was to grow and eventually achieve preeminent and model form at Harvard, beginning in the 1870s under the deanship of Christopher Langdell (Stevens, 1971, pp. 414, 415, 423, 426). Thus too, women's disappearance from law coincided with the symbiotic growth of formal legal education and the legal profession as a powerful ruling class in the United States.

As policy advisers and technicians of change, lawyers became an entrenched aristocratic meritocracy. With law as an organized profession, the power of lawyers was now more closely held than ever, and admission to practice was regulated, either by statutes or by the courts themselves, in a manner designed possessively and self-servingly to preserve its white maleness. Women were affirmatively excluded from legal education as well as from the practice of law. The law school first to open its doors to women was the University of Iowa in 1869, the year that Arabella Babb Mansfield became the first woman to be admitted to the bar (also in Iowa) in United States (Haselmayer, 1969). But as late as 1900 many states still refused to admit women to both bar and law school (Pettus, 1900).

In 1869, the year Belle Mansfield was admitted to the Iowa bar, Myra Bradwell passed a most creditable examination but was denied admission to the bar by the Supreme Court of Illinois on the ground that she was a married woman, her married status being a disability.[12] Convinced that the real reason had not been given, Bradwell filed an additional brief in forceful opposition, thus compelling the court to articulate the true reason. The court then delivered an elaborate opinion in which it refused to admit Myra Bradwell on the ground that she was a woman.[13] She took her case on a writ of error to the United States Supreme Court, which affirmed the judgment[14] of the Illinois Supreme Court on the ground that the practice of law was not a right protected by the Constitution and that, therefore, a state court could construe whether a woman was entitled to practice law in that state. Mr. Justice Bradley filed his infamous sexist concurrence from which I have already quoted.

---

[12] For information about the life of Myra Bradwell, see "Bradwell v. The State" (1971); "Note—Death of Mrs. Myra Bradwell" (1894); "Note—Myra Bradwell" (1894); Johnson (1964).

[13] See *In re Bradwell* (1894).

[14] See *Bradwell v. Illinois* (1872).

Soon after the Supreme Court decision, Bradwell succeeded in getting the Illinois Legislature to enact a statute granting to all persons, regardless of sex, the freedom to select an occupation or profession. Twenty years later, the judges of the Illinois Supreme Court, on their own motion, directed that a license to practice law be issued to Myra Bradwell, and on March 28, 1892, she was admitted to practice before the Supreme Court of the United States.

Although neither Belle Mansfield nor Myra Bradwell ever practiced law, they were extremely active in public life. Bradwell, especially, was active in feminist causes. She worked for law reform, drafting and procuring the passage of a law establishing a married woman's right to her own earnings, which otherwise would have been the property of her husband. She also won passage of statutes guaranteeing to a widow or widower a share in the deceased spouse's estate.

Since the time that Mansfield and Bradwell broke through the sexual exclusivity of the American legal profession, women's participation in law has continued to meet with resistance from the law school and the organized bar. Thus, even as late as 20 years ago, a report documents that women had not come far in the profession.

Women's status in the legal profession: The 1951 survey

In 1954, Albert P. Blaustein and Charles O. Porter summarized the Survey of the Legal Profession, undertaken in 1947 by an all-male director and council and completed seven years later. In three pages on women, the authors admitted that their book dealt primarily with the 199,052 male members of the bar, because "the nation's 5,059 Portias (2.48 percent of the total) are in a special category . . ." (Blaustein & Porter, 1954, p. 29). Indeed they were in a special category, compared with men, in terms of numbers, opportunities for practice, and public relations within the profession. As Blaustein and Porter reported, the majority of large law offices refused (short of war) to interview women for jobs; women had to work twice as hard as men for half the pay; and relatively few women had won positions of real distinction in practice (private or governmental) or on the bench. The slight percentage of women in the legal profession reflected—as it reflects today—women's uphill struggle for professional education, opportunity, and recognition in the law.

Universities made it almost impossible for women to obtain an adequate legal education. Although Michigan admitted women law students in 1870, Yale in 1886, and Cornell in 1887, they were the exceptions: Columbia barred women until 1929 and Harvard, the preeminent and model institution, until 1950. In 1951 women still constituted a small percentage of law school classes, between 3 and 4 percent at Cornell, Michigan, Stanford, and Southern California, for example, and about 6 percent at Yale and NYU and 7 percent at Columbia. This underrepresentation of women was not related to inferior ability, for law schools reporting to the survey admitted that women students' aptitude and general record were at least as meritorious as men students'. Cornell disclosed that since it had first admitted women, three of them had been either first in their classes or editors-in-chief of the *Cornell Law Quarterly.* Columbia also indicated that 24 percent of its women law students had maintained A averages, a proportion higher than men's.

In addition to the struggle for legal education, Blaustein and Porter noted women's struggle for admission to bar associations. The American Bar Association excluded women from membership until 1918, and the Association of the Bar of the City of New York held out until 1937. Because women were at first excluded, and because even when they were later permitted membership they were denied participation in the executive and policy-making bodies of the organizations, women formed and maintained their own bar associations, such as the National Association of Women Lawyers, founded in 1899. While women's separate organizations have provided women lawyers with collective support and solidarity, the real work of the organized profession has been maintained within the "regular" bar associations. Because women have organized themselves outside of these powerful centers, women lawyers have remained remote from the source of power, despite the fact that they now can hold membership in all bar associations.

Today the participation of women in the legal profession is changing, and rapidly. The current mass influx of women into law schools and women's vigorous participation in legal reform are harbingers of a change whose nature and scope are as yet unknown.

Presently there is a dramatic increase in the number of women entering law schools. According to Professor Shirley Bysiewicz, the results of a 1972 survey undertaken by the Committee on Women in Legal Education of the Association of American Law Schools (AALS) indicate that 16 percent of entering law students are women.[15] The lowest percentage of women students in the entering class of law schools in 1972–73 was 4 percent, the highest, 46 percent. The overall percentage of women in law schools (all years) has risen to 12.5. This represents an extraordinary increase over the 1966–1970 enrollment for women students (from 4.3 percent to 7.8 percent). In the fall of 1972, 12,272 women were enrolled in 149 American Bar Association–approved law schools, which approximates the total number of women lawyers currently in practice (Trebilcock, 1973). Thus one generation of law school students will double the number of women lawyers in the United States.

Moreover, while the overall number of applicants has increased threefold (from 47,584 in 1969 to 153,282 in 1972), the number of female applicants has risen to 14 times the 1969 figure. Although in 1969–70, 44 percent of all applicants were offered a place in law school, this figure fell to 18 percent in 1972–73. The acceptance rate for women, however, did not correspondingly decline during this same period, dropping only from 55 to 43 percent. The statistics suggest that although law schools are incrementally expanding, they are, nevertheless, admitting fewer men.[16] Women, however, still constitute only 7.4 percent of the total number of applicants. Bysiewicz notes that the acceptance rate of female applicants in 1972–73 was 43 percent compared to the overall 18 percent acceptance rate for that year, but adds that this is due to the relatively small number of female

[15] Eighty-one of the 124 AALS-accredited law schools contacted responded to a four-part questionnaire, which contained sections on recruitment and admissions, faculty, placement, and intraschool policies. The questionnaire covered the academic years 1969–70 to 1972–73.

[16] The Carnegie Commission on Higher Education confirms this in *Opportunities for Women in Higher Education* (1973, p. 101). It reports that the number of applications, rather than the number of enrollments, has risen dramatically; and law schools have responded cautiously in increasing the number of student places available. The 1972 total freshman enrollment in law schools was actually reported to be down 3 percent from the previous year.

applicants and predicts that as the number of female applications increases, the percentage of female acceptances will decline, creating a pattern similar to male applicants.[17]

Although these figures indicate a steady increase of women enrolling in law schools, the highest figure is still only 16 percent of all law students. The relationship of this new population to change in the law school will not be simple or direct, in part because the student body is not the prime mover in the law school, and in part because the interrelationship of society and law, the legal profession, and the law school is extremely complex.

The legal profession determines the complexion of the law school population as well as the curriculum. Supply and demand govern their relationship in much the same way that law responds to the particular needs of society, which law itself defines (through grants of power, right, privilege, duty, liability, and immunity) as capitalist and patriarchal. The largest percentage of course offerings relate to private property and business and corporate interests, and their content reflects generally the preferential status of men over women in order to prepare lawyers to be the engineers and servants of a form of social organization based upon the acquisition of personal wealth and the maintenance of male power. Thus the class of persons that controls the law is also the class that controls society by employing law to serve the very basic economic, political, and social institutions created in the first instance through the use of legal power. Law is to society, then, as law school is to law. I want to be clear about this sequence, for when I speak of change, it should be understood that I think that the holders of legal power must relinquish it (voluntarily or not) before new legal forms can be created and legal education can change.

But whatever the form, legal education and law stand together in an absolute relationship. In no realistic sense, then, should we think that simply by initiating changes in law school can we

---

[17] Professor Bysiewicz reports that the Law School Aptitude Test (LSAT) averages of the entering law school class have risen from 554 in 1969–70 to 606 for 1972–73. Women entrants' LSAT scores averaged 602. Cumulative undergraduate grade-point averages of female entrants were also about the same as the overall class averages, which rose from 2.79 in 1969–70 to 3.15 in 1972–73. The undergraduate grade average of female entrants was .10 higher than the overall average while their LSAT scores were 4 points lower.

change law; law school is not the vanguard of our legal institutions. Rather, as a supplier, law school responds to the demands of law, and ultimately of those in power. This is not to imply, however, that some important changes cannot and have not occurred in law school, for education can and does change people's attitudes and consciousness. But the impact of these changes upon law itself will be indirect, affecting future lawyers who may, as the holders of power, affect law itself. As law school is the training camp for future generations of lawyers, lawmakers, and judges, feminist consciousness raising within law school is therefore of some importance.

I see law school not only as a feeder of the legal profession's needs, but also as a receptor, reflector, and transmitter of its values. Indeed elite law schools see themselves this way, viewing the three-year period of legal education as a period of intense and all-consuming indoctrination into legal values, thought, and method. Thus, for example, outside employment is discouraged: courses for the first year, and often for the second and third years as well, are deliberately scheduled through the week between 8 A.M. and 6 P.M. to ensure unavailability of unchopped blocks of time in which one might work part time or devote oneself to another interest. An attitude that views a total time (life) commitment as prerequisite to legal education is thus used to justify the prohibition of part-time study in most major, accredited law schools. Because most legal educators feel that to be *effective,* legal education must occur in an environment of intense concentration, the law school presents itself as a microcosm of law. It is not surprising, then, to find that law school, like law, is itself misogynist.

If this is so, why then should a woman go to law school? And once there, why should she waste her energy working for change? The answers, I think, are relatively simple. Women should go to law school to become lawyers, because to be a lawyer is to have power, and significant structural change can only be accomplished, if at all, from the inside of law and through law's own mechanisms—for only lawyers (later they become judges) and legislators (mostly all are lawyers) can change law. Women, then, by becoming lawyers, perhaps can gain control over, and redress, their own debased, male-imposed status.

Further, law schools must be made to respond to women's

needs while they are students and to provide women with the legal tools related to their own self-interest and reconstruction of their status. And while this process occurs, the consciousness of men in law schools may also be raised.

At this point in time law is the domain of men, a men's club, if you will. This attitude permeates the law school, where it is clear that women are regarded as invaders of an exclusive male territory and as challengers of men's preeminence there. Most men, unsure of what to make of this sudden invasion, respond with hostility; others respond with condescension. All are aware of the threat in this respect: we may be entering a period when the supply of lawyers has met, even exceeded, the demand, and good jobs are becoming scarcer every day. Most men must now share the already slim pickings with women, who for the most part are tough competition.

Although it seems to me to be increasingly difficult not to take women law students seriously, the idea does still prevail that some if not all of us have merely taken husband-hunting one step further. I remember vividly the shock and disgust I felt when, as a first-year law student in the law library, my attention was distracted from my contracts book by an unknown male asking, incredulously, "Do you intend to practice law?" "Well," I replied too graciously (I have since learned how not to respond at all to such questions), "I am certainly not here for the sake of my health or for the aesthetic enhancement of my life."

When I entered law school in 1969, many women students were as alienated as I by a pervasive classroom attitude that considered the entire student body, legal profession, indeed the world, to be male. Male professors often ignored the presence of women by addressing the class as "Gentlemen." Or they used illustrations insulting to women: "A system of procedure is just like a woman; if you've seen one you've seen them all." Or as a professor in a course on corporations said, calling on a male student, "Suppose you *guys* want to start a 6-*man* firm. How would you form the partnership?"

Today, through the consciousness raising that women have done in law schools across the country, such blatant classroom sexism is disappearing. Moreover, standard derogatory female stereotypes so frequently used in the past by professors as stock characters, auxiliary players to male central characters in illustrative hypotheticals (the traditional method of legal education), are reportedly less in vogue: the helpless widow, the dependent wife, the deceptive bitch, the pure virgin, the irrational or hysterical female, the silly consumer who is easily conned by male exploiters, the rape victim who secretly wanted to be raped, or any stupid loathsome creature. The hissing revolt of women students has deprived professors of the demonstration of sexist wit.[18] At least in law school such "wit" is now unpopular and is being replaced at least by basic courtesy, if not by solidarity or raised consciousness.

Women's associations and conferences
Changes in professorial behavior, including a new deference to women's dignity as well as other changes that are occurring in law schools across the country, have been stimulated by the organized efforts of women law students. Although some groups are more organized and effective than others, and although some have opened membership to all law school–based women rather than to women law students only, possibly as many as 70 percent of the law schools have a women's association (Bysiewicz, 1973). Often described formally in the law school catalog, such associations have "in addition to working on projects connected with curriculum change, placement and recruitment . . . held orientation sessions for new female law students . . . " (Bysiewicz, 1973, p. 512).

Two such women's associations have been particularly effective in organized efforts. At Berkeley, the Boalt Hall Women's Association (BHWA), for example, has an excellent recruitment program. In addition to a poster reading "Wanted by the Law: Women," which it has distributed widely, the BHWA has placed notices in many periodicals announcing "a nationwide recruitment project to encourage women to enter the field of law." To

[18] Analogous wit may still be found in medical schools. Professors use slides of pinup girls to enliven their lectures: THE END written across naked female buttocks at the close of a slide series. Other examples are grotesquely cruel: breezy tango music accompanies a motion picture demonstrating a crippled woman's jerky gait; a dying woman's emaciated body and huge swollen belly call for the following professorial words—"Now, this is Bubbles, and as you look into her lovely eyes. . . ." For further examples, see Smith (1973) and Frankfort (1973).

support its work, the association has prepared three booklets: "How to Apply to Law School," "Wanted by the Law: Women," and "California's Law Schools" (a guide).

In 1970, 14 members of the Law Women's Caucus of the University of Chicago Law School filed a pioneer complaint with the Equal Employment Opportunities Commission (EEOC), alleging that the law school's employment service engaged in unlawful employment practices in violation of Title VII of the Civil Rights Act of 1964 by operating an employment service that tolerated and supported discriminatory recruiting and hiring practices of law firms. The case has extremely important implications for women students at every law school because most law schools permit law firms to use law school facilities to recruit employees, in spite of the fact that the firms often grant only perfunctory interviews to women students and refuse to hire women on an equal basis with men. Law firms commonly use such excuses as "We had a woman once but she left to get married" or "We would like to hire women but there are a couple of senior partners who won't stand for it." I was once told in an interview on law school territory, "Our firm is just not ready to hire women."[19] As at Chicago, the placement services often receive letters from firms specifically requesting men, and the services attempt to fill these job orders.

As a result of the complaint by the Law Women's Caucus, the EEOC issued a landmark decision on June 19, 1972. It ruled that a law school discriminates against women students and graduates when it cooperates with law firms that do not hire women on an equal basis with men, and that the law school's employment service has an obligation to act affirmatively to eliminate discriminatory practices of employers using their facilities. The University of Chicago Law School then had two choices: to comply or to file suit in federal court. Instead, however, accord-

---

[19] Professor Shirley Bysiewicz reports that at 40 percent of the 77 law schools with organized placement offices to assist students in obtaining employment, incidents of alleged discrimination against women job applicants have been reported: "The most prevalent form of discrimination reported was the type of questions asked of women by job interviewers. Almost half of the complaints involved allegations of discriminatory personal questions such as, 'Do you plan to have children?' or 'Are you on the pill?' There were also complaints of alleged outright refusals to consider female applicants as well as complaints of alleged statements made by interviewers that salary, promotion prospects or work assignments would be different for women" (Bysiewicz, 1973, pp. 509–510).

ing to Karen Kaplowitz, who was one of the charging parties in the Law Women's Caucus and who now practices law in Los Angeles, the law school moved to request that the commission reconsider its decision. On November 12, 1973, in a most irregular and unprecedented action, the commission reversed its prior ruling and dismissed the charge on the ground that "there was no reasonable cause to believe that the charge of discrimination was true."[20] Kaplowitz says that Law Women's Caucus is planning to sue both the University of Chicago Law School and the EEOC in federal court. The caucus had not been formally informed of the reversed ruling and had learned of its existence only accidentally.

In addition to intralaw school women's associations, women law students have been holding national conferences on Women and the Law since 1969 (when the first national conference was held in New York), with regional conferences in between.[21] Each year the conference as a whole votes on the host law school for the following year from among those schools "bid" for by their women representatives. The national and regional conferences have provided the germinal structure out of which unified feminist strategy and theory have emerged. Organized outside the law school structure, the conferences have had a visible and direct impact on the legal education establishment. It is important, therefore, to examine the content of these conferences, for they have provided the source of women law students' power.

Although the particular focus and politics have differed from conference to conference, three main purposes are served: (1) to become personally acquainted with each other and develop a sense of group solidarity; (2) to exchange information about the problems women incur at particular law schools and to report on the remedial progress being made; (3) through workshops, to develop and educate women law students in areas of law which, though of particular concern to women, are systematically deleted from regular course content. The development of women's curriculum at the grass roots level, where it is often self-taught outside the formal law school curriculum, has slowly been infused into the law school curriculum through a vigorous

[20] See EEOC Decision, 72–2041, Case No. YCH1–409, June 19, 1972, and EEOC Decision on Reconsideration, 74–30, Case No. YCH1-409, November 12, 1973.

[21] For a history of the national conferences, see Goodman (1974, p. 1).

movement begun at national conferences. This movement has been generated by women returning to their individual law school with a strategy and inspiration directed toward the development of courses on Women and the Law. I shall return to this subject later, but it is important to recognize that this movement of women law students has been effective in influencing the legal educational establishment: by October 1972, the New York University School of Law and the Association of American Law Schools (AALS) cosponsored a two-day Symposium on Law School Curriculum and the Legal Rights of Women, which was funded with grants from the Ford Foundation and the Rockefeller Family Fund. The symposium held a series of panels on constitutional law, taxation, criminal law, family law, property law, and labor law that presented to law professors research in these areas and suggested curriculum changes. Further, the annual AALS meeting now includes a Committee on Women in Legal Education. I want to parenthetically note here, and will return to this point later, that at the 1971 Women and Law Conference at Yale, there was apprehension among the women students that the 1972 AALS Symposium was an attempt by AALS to stem and even coopt the growing movement for separate women and the law courses by quickly integrating this material into regular curricula, thereby removing the development of women's course material from the control of women and vesting it in the regular faculty, thus also depriving women law students of their key focus for organized action. But, as it turned out, the intent of the AALS was to stimulate inclusion of women's law in the regular courses *and* also to retain the specialized Women and the Law course to maximize student exposure to this important area. Later, I shall discuss the issue of integration of this material into regular courses, how it is to be done, and who is to do it.

The national and regional Women and the Law conferences have reflected the wide diversity in feminist consciousness that exists among women law students and lawyers. While all agree that women's rights is an important concern, there is disagreement about the nature of women's class oppression and about which issues should receive priority attention. The women at the 1971 Yale conference identified heavily with the class of women they felt was most oppressed by the law—poor women whose lives were hopelessly entangled in the debasing and discriminatory welfare and criminal justice systems—and accordingly many workshops focused on these matters.

Also of concern was the development of a textbook for Women and the Law courses, as none existed then and the few courses that were then being taught used informal materials. A casebook, as legal textbooks are called, would legitimate the subject matter itself and allow women at law schools more readily to convince the faculty that courses in women and the law should be added to the curriculum. Because conveners of the Yale conference had a grant for a casebook, conference discussion focused on its content, emphasis, and politics. Although that book is still in the preparatory stage, two other casebooks on women and the law are now available.

The 1972 conference held at Berkeley's Boalt Hall was concerned with forms of practice alternative to the big, male top-heavy law firms. Workshops centered on legal collectives and all-women law firms. There was also a strong presence of lesbians, as there was again at the 1974 annual conference in Austin, and, consequently, workshops were held on the legal oppression of lesbians as well as on the relationship between women lawyers and lesbians and between lesbians and heterosexual women.

The major effects of women's law school associations and conferences have been felt in two areas: the recruitment and hiring of women faculty, and the development of courses supplementing the law school curriculum. In the fall of 1969 most major law schools had none or one woman on their faculties, and law relevant to women's interests and legal status was not part of the curriculum. Now, in 1975, most law schools have been prompted by their organized women students to make affirmative efforts to hire women faculty, and courses in Women and the Law have emerged everywhere.

Women as law professors

Opportunities for Women in Higher Education (Carnegie Commission, 1973) reports that women have been almost absent from law school faculties. In 1968–70 women constituted only 28 (or 1.6 percent) of the faculty members in 38 leading law schools, and only 7 of these 28 women were full professors. Between 1970 and 1972 the proportion of women professors listed in the AALS

Directory rose from 3.1 to 5.6 percent. (The *Directory* lists librarians and certain administrators as well as faculty members.)

According to Bysiewicz (1973), in the 81 law schools responding to the 1972 AALS survey, 8 percent of the deans were women and 8 percent of all faculty members were women, twice the percentage reported in 1970. Most of these new women faculty members, however, were hired at low faculty rank: the percentage of instructors increased from 16 percent in 1970 to 23 percent in 1972; full professors, from 2.39 percent to 2.54 percent.[22]

While more than 70 percent of law schools have affirmative action programs for the purpose of seeking qualified female (and minority-group) faculty, administrators, and other personnel, most schools discourage part-time appointments, and part-time appointees have fewer faculty rights and privileges and are often reappointed annually without tenure. Fifteen schools provide part-time faculty appointments for faculty members whose child-care responsibilities prevent them from accepting full-time positions, or for those who are full-time attorneys and part-time professors. At only 10 percent of the schools were part-time faculty members eligible for promotion or tenure.

In addition to the barriers restricting women whose child-care responsibilities limit them to part-time faculty positions, I have found that, in seeking to implement affirmative action programs, law schools distinctly favor those women who most closely resemble the typical male faculty member and disfavor active feminist women candidates. Although research and writing are two significant criteria for hiring and promotion, feminist legal scholarship is regarded with little interest, and on occasion, with suspicion or hostility. Katherine Brinkman of the University of Cincinnati School of Law, for example, reports that the women's association brought sufficient pressure on the law faculty to gain its commitment to hire a woman, "if it could find a qualified one." When the women's association found a candidate for the post who had all the traditional academic credentials—law review, Order of the Coif (honorary society), and clerkship to an appellate judge, in addition to several scholarly publications in legal journals—and who was an acknowledged feminist, the

---

[22] While only 1 percent of male faculty hold the lowest rank of instructor, 11 percent of the women faculty have this rank. Moreover, the survey indicates that while 49 percent of the male faculty have tenure, only 21 percent of the women do.

Cincinnati Law School refused to grant her an interview and instead invited two nonfeminist women candidates they had discovered. In choosing between those two, the preference of women law students was ignored. Thus, although some law schools are now actively seeking women faculty members, the kind of women they prefer may constitute a subtle refinement of their traditional discrimination against women in faculty appointments.

The Women and the Law course

The AALS 1972 survey revealed that half of all law schools now offer a course on Women and the Law and others offer a seminar on this subject. The first courses were organized in 1968 or 1969 by women students who realized that professors were not ready to admit the study of women and the law into generic and appropriate areas. So it was at several law schools simultaneously and independently that women began to form special classes to study their own legal status. The effort arose as much out of students' ignorance of the laws and cases that affect women's lives as it did out of their particular feminist consciousness and political strategy. From the start, many conceived of the course as serving dual objectives: education and internal organization.

I shall describe the effort made at the University of California, Los Angeles, not only because it was the movement I was personally involved in, but also because its aims and procedures were not unique. Moreover, in retrospect, recalling the accounts given by other women at national conferences, I think it was an unusually successful effort, partly because UCLA is more receptive than other law schools to student initiative.

Although we were not wholly certain about what we wanted, we did have several concrete objectives. First, we wanted a course called "Women and the Law," which we conceived of as a structured way to come together and analyze at least the one aspect of women's oppression that was within our immediate grasp and to gain some basic skills, essential to the woman lawyer interested in litigating women's issues and serving women's legal needs. Second, we wanted to begin original scholarship that would become the bedrock of a collection of women's materials on permanent reserve in the law library. To that end, we gathered briefs, complaints, and manuscripts as well as published materials that would be useful in women's studies and litigation. The law library was extremely helpful in our effort to gather and catalog materials. Third, we wanted to build a political base in the law school that could serve as an ongoing organization that would work for such goals as fair admissions standards for women, the hiring of women faculty, and the improvement of women's physical facilities.

Since no prepared casebooks or other materials were available, the first step was to prepare some. We eventually produced a multilithed book[23] of articles and cases organized under the following table of contents:

I. The Suffrage Movement: Legal Change and Feminism

II. Constitutional Status

III. Family and Welfare Law

    A. Illegitimacy

    B. Marriage

    C. Same-Sex Marriage

    D. Legal Relations and the Family

    E. Divorce and Child Custody

    F. Community Property

    G. Welfare and Family Law

    H. Child Care

IV. Control of Our Bodies

    A. Abortion

    B. Female Sexuality

    C. Woman-Defined Woman

    D. Birth Control

    E. Artificial Insemination

    F. Sterilization

V. Criminal Law

    A. Prostitution

    B. Rape

---

[23] This book's only surviving value is as an historical document, for it is outdated and sketchy, and has been superseded by two new casebooks on Women and the Law and a third that is forthcoming.

    C. Statutory Rape

    D. Women in Prison

    E. Parole

    F. Juvenile Women

VI. Labor and Employment

    A. Economic Background

    B. Equal Pay Act of 1963

    C. Executive Order 11246

    D. State Protective Legislation

    E. Title VII of the 1964 Civil Rights Act

    F. Women and the Unions

    G. The Work We Ignore: Prostitution, Housework, Welfare

    H. Other Countries: Soviet Union and Sweden

    I. Unemployment Benefits

VII. Media: Images and Legal Strategies

The second step was steering the course proposal through the curriculum committee and to the faculty for approval as a student-taught course with a faculty sponsor.

As law students who had fully absorbed legal teaching methods, we proceeded to create a course, not surprisingly, that focused in a typically uncreative, detached, and structured way chiefly on laws, cases, and legal doctrines pertinent to women. The result was insufficient contact with real visceral issues and feelings and an overstructured intellectualism. Although we gained knowledge about sex discrimination from statistical and case analyses, we did not, during that pilot course, gain profound understanding of our own or other women's oppression. Each year since then, however, the course in Women and the Law at UCLA has changed substantially in organization and approach, style, and method, according to the vision and demands of its participants.

Beyond UCLA, the effort to gain recognition for these courses as legitimate features of the curriculum has been moderately successful. Some law schools have refused academic credit for courses in Women and the Law but allow it to be taught on a no-credit basis. Some schools have hired women lawyers as lecturers especially to teach this one course. But the tokenism is obvious and indicates that Women and the Law is still not a fully respected discipline of law. Women who specialize in it, moreover, are not fully qualified for professorships, and must show some other "legitimate" expertise. This means, of course, that feminist lawyers most committed to the women's legal struggle are those least likely to be hired.

It is important to recognize that while it appears we are making significant inroads through the addition of Women and the Law to the law curriculum, in fact a good deal of deception is involved. The status of the course itself is inferior to that of "real" law courses, and women lawyers who put women's courses as their first priority in teaching expertise have a rough time getting hired on law faculties. In fact, feminist women law students and lawyers who desire careers in legal education are being indirectly channeled away from specializing in areas of law important to women. One well-meaning woman law professor once confided to a feminist student who was committed to a teaching career that a heavily feminist publication record would not help in obtaining a teaching position because feminist publications on women's law are not considered "hard" areas valued by male professors, regardless of their analytical or scholarly character. In fact, feminist publications can hurt rather than help women obtain academic positions solely because of their subject matter. Thus even the "publish or perish" ethic prevalent in most academic institutions applies a double standard to women and feminist scholarship.

An important concern is whether courses in Women and the Law will survive as separate entities and as focal points for feminist activity, identification, and thought in the law schools. Since the sudden appearance in 1969 of such courses, many law professors have responded to the complaint that women's law is omitted from standard courses, and an organized effort has been made, under the sponsorship of the Association of American Law Schools, to integrate women's law into its natural fields. I think this is an important thing to do, because it will result in the exposure of *all* students to women's law. But it is absolutely essential that this integration not be understood as an alternative to the course in Women and the Law and the various in-depth seminars on specific women's issues it has engendered, nor be used as justification to delete women's courses and seminars from the curriculum on the ground that the subject matter is covered elsewhere. The functions of women's courses in the law

school—to educate in a feminist perspective, to encourage original scholarship on women's law, to provide a base for organizing
other projects, and simply to support female students in a male
world—are functions that cannot be served by integrating wom-
en's materials into the regular curriculum. To do so would
transfer to men exclusively the responsibility for educating
women about women, since most standard courses are still
taught by men, whereas from the start almost every Women and
the Law course has been taught by a woman, whether student,
lawyer hired for the purpose, or the rare female professor. What
I hope will happen, therefore, is that women's law will be
broadly integrated throughout the law school curriculum, and
that women's courses and seminars will be retained as well.

I think that feminists are needed on law faculties to teach both
regular courses and women's courses in a manner that offsets the
male-dominated ambience of law schools and the male-centered
interpretation of the law. If the limit of change possible in law
schools precludes hiring many strong feminists, then it will be
reasonable for women to consider the alternative of separate,
all-women or women-controlled law schools. Indeed, as I shall
discuss shortly, such separatism may be essential to equal
educational opportunity. Before moving on to the subject of
equal educational opportunity, however, I want to mention two
crucial programmatic changes that are overdue in legal
education—part-time study and child care—and to conclude by
discussing more generally the question of feminist consciousness
in the law school.

Part-time study and child care

The Carnegie Commission on Higher Education (1973, p. 106)
notes in *Opportunities for Women in Higher Education* that
"probably the most important factor tending to discriminate
against women in admission to graduate study is a variety of
rules and informal policies discouraging admission of students
who wish to study on a part-time basis." A lack of part-time
study programs for women who must work while attending law
school and for women who have child-care and domestic responsibilities is a major barrier to women's entrance into law and
other professional schools. Obviously such women compete at a
disadvantage with men students whose wives or girlfriends
either support them financially or care for their households and
children.

Part-time study is a volatile subject in "first-rate" law schools, meaning accredited schools without opportunity for nighttime enrollment. While many members of law school faculties recognize that recruitment of women students is a priority, only a few acknowledge that equal educational opportunity requires that part-time study be available for otherwise qualified women who are excluded from the class of potential law students because of economic and domestic responsibilities. If recruitment of women is a sincere priority, part-time study must follow. Probably the issue of part-time study will provide the decisive battleground for women law students' struggle for self-determination and equal educational opportunity. I shall not be surprised if this battle will be lost because of the vehement resistance offered by law faculties in their efforts to maintain control over their professional institutions.[24]   Basically, the problem could be characterized as one of conflict of interest. True, many professors agree that a part-time program is of vital importance to women and equal accessibility to law school is dependent upon it. Yet at the same time it is hardly likely that a law school will voluntarily demote itself to a part-time institution. Within the pecking order of institutions for the study of law, part-time and night schools (the ones that best accommodate working class persons) hold the lowest status, whereas full-time law schools enjoy the aristocratic reputation characteristic of elite educational institutions. There is thus a basic contradiction between the desire to open up the law school to those traditionally excluded from it and the desire of members of elite institutions to protect their own status, which is tied to the status of the institution with which they are associated. This fundamental class structure of our education system must be recognized and dealt with as it directly relates to the accessibility of "first-rate" education to women and other deprived persons.

Law schools, I think, are willing to do something, but not to become part-time *institutions* in which all persons who meet the entrance requirements could attend on a part-time basis. They

---

[24] Columbia Law School has recently adopted a resolution allowing students who have primary responsibility for child care to attend part time. The issue was raised at Columbia when the wife of a faculty member sought the right to be a part-time student. Interestingly, the one woman allowed to attend UCLA Law School part time was also the wife of a (non–law school) faculty member. UCLA abandoned the principle immediately after admitting her. Women at UCLA Law School hope to use Columbia as a precedent with which to reopen the issue.

may eventually permit part-time *programs* for a limited number of students who would be selected on the basis of certain eligibility criteria. Whether law faculties could even agree on those criteria and find rational and justifiable standards by which to limit the class of eligible persons is uncertain. If, for example, women with children were to be included, should men with children, or men working full time, and nonwhites also be eligible? If not, how can law faculties be made to see why? If they cannot be, inability to agree upon the class of potential part-time law students will become the justification for not initiating even part-time study programs. I have a suspicion, however, that the awesome specter of becoming a *part-time institution* will always engender new excuses for not allowing women to study law on a part-time basis. As women law students have been unsuccessful in changing this fundamental policy, the perpetuation of these institutional methods of discrimination against women continues to deny them equal educational opportunity.

Closely connected with the need of women to choose part-time study is their need for child-care facilities. Of the 81 law schools responding to the 1972 AALS survey (Bysiewicz, 1973) only one law school reported the existence of a day-care center for children of students, faculty, and staff, although 30 percent of the universities queried had established day-care centers that were available to law school members. Nineteen of the 25 law schools that responded to this question had received requests for day-care centers. In most cases the response to these requests had been negative, based upon asserted lack of funds or space and insufficient need to justify such a facility. Although at a few law schools such requests were referred to committees for study and recommendations, only three schools planned to establish a day-care center or to affiliate with one at the university.

The issue of child care and the university has been thoughtfully and adequately discussed in Chapter 1, and there is no need to belabor the issue here. But it merits emphasizing that child care is "one need that is primary if women are to assume any real equality in the academic world, one challenge that the university today, like the society around it, evades with every trick in its possession. . . . While excellent universal early childhood care should be a major priority in any reasonably humane society, the primary and moving impulse behind the children's center would be to help equalize the position of women" (Rich, pp. 34, 38 of this volume).

Feminist consciousness in the law school

To promote a changed curriculum, build a library of materials relevant to women's law, and gain certain forms of institutional flexibility, women law students need to build politically strong women's groups in which all women rigorously participate. The failure of feminists to build such groups is another serious problem. At the initial stage, when law schools were frightened by the mere existence of a women's association, regardless of the size of its membership, and when these same schools were willing to make token concessions without any intent of fundamentally altering legal education to suit women's needs, small and weak women's groups were remarkably effective. Some administrators, reacting out of fear and expediency, did not discover that perhaps only 2 percent of women in law school identified as feminists and were militant in their struggle to make the law school environment more hospitable to all women and to serve women's needs.

The fact is that not all, or even the majority, of women in law school feel insulted, degraded, or outraged by law or by their situations in law school. Most women are committed to succeeding as lawyers, not as women lawyers, and do not identify with feminist programs or consciousness. As law school administrators and faculties come to realize this, they may become less responsive to militant women's demands, because administrators and faculties will soon see that they have little to lose through resistance, and only their own closely held power to lose through cooperation.

It is deeply disturbing to see women law students seek self-promotion in terms of the status, prestige, and achievement obtainable through emulation of old-style male law careers. This phenomenon somewhat negates the hypothesis that through women's leadership and the infusion into law of those female values that have traditionally differentiated women from men—nurturance, harmony, warmth, patience, intuition, emotionality, and ability to mediate—basic institutional changes in law can be obtained. The means that men have used to resolve conflicts—violence and war on the one hand, the adversary system on the other—are not suitable to women because these means destroy.

If women will not be content to war abroad or to fight as adversaries in courts of law, then will not their ascendence into power change the very method of resolving conflicts, change the nature of law itself? This change, however, is dependent upon *widespread* feminist awakening, which has not yet occurred in law schools. It was women who were feminists before coming to law school who have mainly been the ones committed to organizing other women and raising feminist consciousness in the law school.[25]

My present view of the paucity of feminist consciousness in women law students is open to the criticism that it lacks any far-reaching feminist analysis, and that it does not take into account the fact that the socialization of women to accept their token position—and to think of themselves as "special" at the price of never challenging the system that rewards them—has been just another version of the same process that socializes other women to remain pliant and passive in low-status jobs.[26] If I despair too easily of these women, I am also mindful that unless we can reach out to highly trained, often brilliant women and believe in their capacity for change, we will lose a great source of potential strength for the movement. Just as we must avoid falling into the trap of thinking of law as so fossilized that

---

[25] The consciousness of some male students and professors has been moved by feminists. Adrienne Rich has observed, however, that the men have far less to lose in a short-run sense and thus take far fewer risks than the women by supporting feminism. She writes in a letter: "Women are always being splintered from each other by our long acculturation in self-hatred and mutual mistrust; why not work harder with the women instead of writing them off in favor of the men who will always hold power as long as women remain divided?"

[26] Mary Daly (in *Beyond God the Father: Toward a Philosophy of Women's Liberation*) speaks to my expressed doubts when she writes: "There are some who persist in claiming that the liberation of women will only mean that new characters will assume the same old roles, and that nothing will change essentially in structures, ideologies and values. This supposition is often based on the observation that the very few women in 'masculine' occupations often behave as men do. This kind of reasoning is not at all to the point, for it fails to take into account the fact that tokenism does not change stereotypes or social systems but works to preserve them, since it dulls the revolutionary impulse. The minute proportion of women in the U.S. who occupy such roles (as senators, judges, business executives, doctors, etc.) have been trained by men in institutions defined and designed by men, and they have been pressured subtly to operate according to male rules. There are no alternate models. As sociologist Alice Rossi has suggested, this is not what the women's movement in its most revolutionary potential is all about" (Daly, 1973, p. 14).

change is impossible, so we must not think of these women as fossilized either.

My pessimism notwithstanding, if fundamental legal change is to occur at all, it will occur from within the institution, and it will require a new breed of lawyers. Although both female and male lawyers have a class interest in power and privilege, because the nature of law as I have described it contains inevitably greater contradictions for women, women may be more likely to become that new breed of lawyers who transform law from within. Even though this transformation is unlikely to occur until women lawyers constitute a sizable percentage of the bar, many agree that as the numbers of feminist women lawyers increase, the probability of their fundamentally changing our legal institutions will increase proportionately. In a letter dated October 24, 1973, Professor Marjorie Fine Knowles of the University of Alabama School of Law writes:

I think my belief that women entering the bar will have a profound impact on the bar is a manifestation of my belief that there does, in fact, exist a woman's culture in this society and that that culture embodies values that are more humane than those of the ruling culture. To the extent that women law students are carriers of that separate culture, they will inject it into the legal practice and that cannot help but have a profound impact on the legal system as we know it. The humane values to which I refer would include a great sensitivity to the needs of others, an awareness of the forces of sexism and probably racism, since the parallels are so close in our society, coupled with an alertness to the mythology by which so many of our decision-makers seem to guide their lives. Once a woman perceives some of the truths about her own position in life, the way she was brought up, and the things that have happened to other women around her because of the way our culture operates on women, I don't think she could be the same and she could certainly never be the same as a man who has not had that experience of heightened consciousness. Some people have raised the question of why women in the profession have not behaved any differently than men up to now, and I believe that one older study shows this to be true. I think probably it is because the women who went through law school prior to any slight emergence of a women's movement either did not have the benefit of the perceptions that movement has brought to us or could not find ways to express their different viewpoints. Now that there are many ways to practice law, including public interest law, I think that women entering the profession will have both the know-how and the added perceptions that will lead them to explore the new avenues which the 60's opened up for lawyers. I think the feminist lawyers will be the ones to take the most advantage of those opportunities.[27]

In the meantime, even while recognizing the present improbability of a few feminist lawyers fundamentally changing our legal institutions, I can still justify the activities in law schools of small militant feminist groups. Law schools need a movement that will raise women's consciousness about their position in a patriarchal culture, challenge the misogyny that pervades all our institutions, lend collective support to women in their daily struggle against a hostile environment, and fight for such basic civil rights as legal equality, equal access to education and employment, control over women's sexual and reproductive lives, and the availability of adequate child-care facilities. In the law school these are all legitimate ends in themselves, regardless of the long-range success or failure of a revolution in the institution of law.

EQUAL EDUCATIONAL OPPORTUNITY   All these observations lead me to the conclusion that, at least as far as women are concerned, equal educational opportunity requires much more than merely "integrating" professional schools by permitting qualified women to enroll in heretofore male territories. In order to achieve equal educational opportunity a concept of equality must be accepted that does not denote parity of treatment, but rather parity of opportunity. Parity of opportunity, as I presently see it, involves inequality of treatment among women and men students in that women are treated preferentially.

The concept of equal educational opportunity for women includes compensatory measures to make up for past discrimination and to bring the class discriminated against up to the level of competitive advantage that the favored class has. But I want to suggest that with respect to women it will involve more than the high concentration of educational resources in the direction of women, coupled with the abolition of the tracking system, to put

---

[27] Examples of feminist lawyers forging new avenues of law practice are already apparent in the form of all-women law firms that deal with or specialize in women's rights: in New York, Bellamy, Blank, Goodman, Kelly, Ross, and Stanley and Lefcourt, Kraft, and Libow; in San Francisco, Davis, Dunlap, and Williams. Some of these women left prestigious Wall Street law firms to create new forms of legal practice, thus rejecting the male route to success.

women in a position of equal educational opportunity where no further preferential treatment would be necessary and neutral treatment of women and men students would no longer be discriminatory against women. This is because the limitations imposed upon women's educational opportunity involve more than the exclusion of women from institutions of higher education or the colonization of women in inferior "separate but equal" institutions. Even if women faced no affirmative (as distinguished from de facto) discrimination in terms of exclusion or underrepresentation in institutions of higher education, and even if women as a class were compensated for the negative effects of a tracking system that ensures that they will be emotionally, academically, and aspirationally disadvantaged, and even if the tracking system itself were abolished, there still would remain the situational disabilities of womanhood itself, the limitations consequent to the inferior role men have imposed upon women and perpetuated through sexist socialization. The domestic servitude and child-care functions that women freely provide to society at such devastating personal cost must be assumed by society itself before women will have equal opportunity for life. This change, however, is so fundamental that it requires nothing less than the total transformation of economic, legal, and social institutions. In the meantime, equal educational opportunity requires that professional schools assume responsibility for the needs of the women students whom these schools are actively recruiting by providing help in whatever means are necessary, such as part-time study, child care, and many feminist women professors. Indeed it is only *after* the professional schools have opened their doors to women that their duty to implement equal educational opportunity begins.

The satisfaction of this duty necessarily entails according women different (preferential) treatment from men. In other words, it requires that classifications be made on the basis of sex that accord one sex, women, benefits that are not accorded to the other sex. Women are thus in the anomalous position of requiring that distinctions be made on the basis of sex, a position contrary to that which women have for decades urged upon the courts: it is counter to the incipient doctrine that sex is a suspect classification that requires an extraordinary justification to satisfy the Fourteenth Amendment's equal protection clause. Now the very doctrine we have championed, that sex is an inherently suspect classification, has in a sense become a detriment to women in that it may well forbid that preferential treatment of women necessary to provide them equal educational opportunity.[28]

For years men have used the category of sex to create, maintain, and justify male-dominated institutions. Because this monster classification was used to discriminate against women, we have tried to kill it, and have at least mutilated it. Now, however, if women's needs require, for example, excluding men from a Women and the Law class, or instituting child care and part-time study for women only, these practices may well be unlawful insofar as they are based upon a suspect classification—sex. What I want to argue is that the emergent constitutional concept of sex equality, which is one of parity and thus requires treating each sex identically, is in conflict with the modern concept of equality, which is measured in terms of equality of *opportunity.* This can be seen clearly in the case where equal educational opportunity requires that women be treated differently from men and yet parity would require identical treatment of women and men. I would suggest, then, that sex-based classifications should be suspect only to prevent men from continuing to maintain public institutions that exclude or otherwise discriminate against women. But sex-based classifications should not be suspect when they are used to provide equal educational opportunity to women who have been victims of past sex discrimination. To require parity now, for the first time, is not a sufficient antibody for the disease of historical misogyny.

Right now I think that equal educational opportunity for women might require an alternative to our present professional schools because these schools have manifested a contempt and scorn for women that is incompatible with the educative process. They abnegate women's history, culture, needs, and identity. They insult women. Most of these schools are calcified like old bones: they are not fertile grounds for the cultivation of women's culture and humanity. The alternatives I envision are (1) the all-women professional school and (2) the women-centered professional school. Perhaps only separatist institutions can

---

[28] But the recent Supreme Court decision in *Kahn v. Shevin* (1974) left open the question whether the presumptive invalidity of sex classifications would preclude benign sex classifications.

be the seedbeds of women's culture where the gathering and creating of women's history may proceed in an atmosphere of warmth and nurturance.

If an all-women professional school is thus essential to women's equal educational opportunity, men must be excluded and the parity concept of equality must yield to equality of opportunity. This principle applies as forcefully to the women-centered professional school. Here, however, men would not necessarily be excluded. They could be students, for example. The essential feature of a women-centered professional school is that women are in control. One thing is quite clear: only if women are in control of their own education can they obtain equal educational opportunity. Only then can women professors neutralize the bias that has permeated male-dominated education. Only then can women students be at home in their education. Only then will the education of women be women's education. The response of professional schools to the presence and demands of women has thus far proved that feminist women cannot fully educate or be educated in male-controlled institutions.[29]

If the Supreme Court ever does declare sex classification, like race classification, to be presumptively invalid under our Constitution, it should be to abolish the history of stigmatization, inferiority, and degradation inflicted upon women by men. But I want to argue, as Professor Askin has argued with respect to

---

[29] The concept of equality that I have been discussing here applies to institutions other than education. All-women law firms, emerging in several major cities now, provide another instance in which women's needs conflict with the concept of parity. The woman-run and woman-staffed law firm is a new phenomenon on the legal scene. It has formed to provide a hospitable working environment for women: often to permit women lawyers and legal workers to dedicate their total energies to practicing women's law and representing women clients, and in some cases, to avoid the usual elitist, class-biased division of labor wherein female secretaries "assist" male attorneys. In the all-women law firm all tasks can be shared by all women working to advance the liberation of women. Of course women's law firms are not all identical, and, for example, where one may accept the basic division between attorney and secretary, another may reject it. Any adequate concept of equality, as applied to the need for all-women law firms, must include the right of all-women law firms to refuse to hire qualified male attorneys, because the liberation of women requires it. At the same time it must forbid all-men law firms to refuse to hire qualified female attorneys. Both of these positions are justifiable as necessary to the eventual attainment of equality by an oppressed and colonized class—women—and until such time as women will have achieved the condition of *real* parity with all men. In the meantime, parity between the sexes is insufficient because it cannot yield equality.

racial classifications, that if this historical and social reality prompts the Supreme Court to declare sex classification presumptively invalid, there is no reason to also say that even those sex classifications that, in fact, operate to remove that stigma and ameliorate the oppression of women are equally pernicious. "There is nothing in law, logic, or morality which requires, as a *neutral* principle, equivalent treatment of oppressor and oppressed" (Askin, 1969, pp. 65, 72–73). If Askin's criterion is applied to the case of compensatory treatment of women, the proper test for such benign sex classification is not the emergent test of presumptive invalidity, but rather the traditional equal protection test of reasonableness of the classification, under which preferential treatment of women would be permissible even though discrimination against women would still be presumptively invalid.[30]

Askin, I, and others are not arguing for a dream but a position that has progressive liberal support. At its April 14–15, 1973, meeting the American Civil Liberties Union adopted a policy statement embodying the principle of affirmative action regarding compensatory treatment and quotas in employment, part of which is herein quoted:

The root concept of the principle of non-discrimination is that individuals should be treated individually, in accordance with their personal merits, achievements and potential, and not on the basis of the supposed attributes of any class or caste with which they may be identified. However, when discrimination—and particularly when discrimination in employment and education—has been long and widely practiced against a particular class, it cannot be satisfactorily eliminated merely by the prospective adoption of neutral, "color-blind" standards for selection among the applicants for available jobs or educational programs. Affirmative action is required to overcome the handicaps imposed by past discrimination of this sort; and, at the present time, affirmative action is especially demanded to increase the employment and the educational opportunities of racial minorities and women.

It should be noted that others, William Van Alstyne (1973, p.1) for example, seek to justify affirmative action plans and preferential hiring by race or sex "not as a patronizing means of

---

[30] Compare *Frontiero v. Richardson* (1973) (plurality opinion, four Justices finding hostile sex classifications *presumptively* invalid) with *Kahn v. Shevin* (1974) (holding valid a benign sex classification).

social redress and not as an abject atonement on a theory of collective guilt, but as an affirmative good in the improvement of the educational institution." His argument for affirmative action is based upon enlightened self-interest in providing for a richer diversity of human resources within an ongoing institution.[31]

CONCLUSION   In these last sentences I want to emphasize briefly just a few points. It is clear to me that without other changes all that mere sex integration of the law school student body will achieve is the creation of a coed student body for whom legal education is unchanged and for whom women's history and culture as an

---

[31] "Improvement in the diversity of the faculty comes out . . . better in every respect as a reason to support the legitimacy of special efforts to reach and to employ women and others. It furnishes an essential nexus with a wholly defensible affirmative objective. In accentuating the positive values of efforts to provide diversity within an institution, moreover, the case for affirmative action is freed of the cant (and difficulties) of 'underutilization,' 'compensation,' 'atonement for past discrimination,' and other baggage which tends to weigh it down. Whether men have been 'underutilized' in higher education, for instance, is quite beside the point in determining whether the Woman's College may wish to consider favoring their appointment to broaden the overall character of its faculty. Whether men may not previously have been employed at that college simply because disproportionately few men thought of it as a desirable place in which to teach (rather than because the College previously discriminated against them) is similarly of no moment; if the new policy is sound, it is not less whatever the explanation of how so few men previously came to be associated with it. Surely, too, the policy may be right and proper without being placed on patronizing terms: as though the interest of the College were merely to give men a better break than it used to give them or than it thinks that 'society' has given them. Rather, the policy stands on its own feet, free of debasing statements about lowering standards for a good cause, giving second-class citizens a leg up, or helping to amortize the national social debt.

"An affirmative action plan is affirmative and admirable exactly as it repudiates such piousness and lays stress, instead, on the positive value of enlightened self-interest in providing for a richer diversity of human resources within an ongoing institution. *E pluribus unum* moved us immensely in the affirmative action of our younger years, and a rather special effort to give it renewed meaning even now still serves as distinguished precept.

"If a general case can be made to reconcile affirmative action plans with the concerns of the ACLU, I believe that it may best be advanced on these terms. Where the ambiance and culture of an institution is felt to be wanting precisely because it appears to provide too much sameness and too little diversity within itself, affirmative action to add persons different in sex or race from those already predominant within the institution is not an invidious reflection upon other persons because of their sex or race, but simply an essential means to widen the character of its staff in a manner it not unreasonably believes to be important" (Van Alstyne, 1973, pp. 10–11).

oppressed people, subjugated by law itself, is denied. History teaches us that oppressors do not gratuitously grant liberty to their oppressed: rather, liberation usually follows some kind of insurrection by the oppressed. This means that the increase in the number of women law students will not be significant unless women who have discovered their feminism and militancy are the majority of that number. It is encouraging that the current trend appears to be a slow but rising tide of militancy and feminism not only among women law students, but among other women professional students.

Long-range changes in the institution of law will function for the benefit of society as a whole as well as for women, for survival's sake, for life's sake. I see women as a significant potential force for restructuring, by humanizing, the basic institutions in society because I think that there is a fundamental difference between women's and men's values. Women's values—those of nurturance, harmony, and grace—are, and women's culture is, different from men's. The only hope for changing the institution of law and other professional institutions from within, therefore, is through the influx of women (and feminized men) into professions. To the extent that we as women can be successful in this endeavor we will be rejecting male-imposed standards of behavior and creating our own more humane and egalitarian standards of behavior.

[I]t is important to keep in focus the fact that in self-liberation women are performing the most effective action possible toward universal human liberation, making available to men the fullness of human being that is lost in sexual hierarchy. To oppose the essential lovelessness of the sexually hierarchical society is the radically loving act. Seen for what it is, the struggle for justice opens the way to a situation in which more genuinely loving relationships are possible (Daly, 1973, p. 51).

REFERENCES

American Civil Liberties Union: "Summary of Actions Taken at April 14–15 Meeting," Apr. 20, 1973.

Askin, Frank: "The Case for Compensatory Treatment," 24 *Rutgers Law Review* 65 (1969).

Blaustein, Albert P., and Charles O. Porter: *The American Lawyer,* The University of Chicago Press, Chicago, 1954.

Bradwell v. Illinois, 83 United States Reports 130 (1872).

"Bradwell v. The State," 1 *Women's Rights Law Reporter* 4 (1971).

Bysiewicz, Shirley: "1972 AALS Questionnaire on Women in Legal Education," 25 *Journal of Legal Education* 503 (1973).

Carnegie Commission on Higher Education: *Opportunities for Women in Higher Education,* McGraw-Hill Book Company, New York, 1973.

Childs, Marjorie M.: "The Women Lawyers Centennial," 59 *American Bar Association Journal* 68 (1970).

Cottle, Marion W.: "The Prejudice against Women Lawyers: How Can It Be Overcome?" *Case and Comment,* vol. 21, no. 5, p. 371, 1914.

Daly, Mary: *Beyond God the Father: Toward a Philosophy of Women's Liberation,* Beacon Press, Boston, 1973.

Davidson, Kenneth, Ruth Ginsberg, and Herma Hill Kay: *Sex-Based Discrimination,* West Publishing Company, St. Paul, Minn., 1974.

Doe v. Bolton, 410 United States Reports 179 (1973).

EEOC Decision, 72–2041, case no. YCH1–409, June 19, 1972.

EEOC Decision on Reconsideration, 74–30, case no. YCH1–409, Nov.12, 1973.

Flexner, Eleanor: *Century of Struggle,* Atheneum Publishers, New York, 1970.

Frankfort, Ellen: *Vaginal Politics,* Bantam Books, Inc., New York, 1973.

Frontiero v. Richardson, 411 United States Reports 677 (1973).

Giles, Isabel: "The Twentieth Century Portia," *Case and Comment,* vol. 21, no. 5, p. 353, 1914.

Goodman, Janice: "Attorney Traces History of Conference," *The Texas Law Forum,* vol. 15, no. 28, p. 1, March 1974.

Graham v. Richardson, 403 United States Reports 365 (1971).

Haselmayer, Louis A.: "Belle A. Mansfield," 55 *Women Lawyers Journal* 46, Spring 1969.

Hoffman, Nancy Jo: "How It Works Out: The Women's Studies Graduate," *Women's Studies Newsletter,* no. 4, p. 3, Summer 1973.

In re Bradwell, 55 Illinois Reports 535 (1869).

In re Paullin, 92 New Jersey Equity Reports 419 (1921).

Johnson, Allen (ed.): "Myra Bradwell," *Dictionary of American Biography,* vol. I, Charles Scribner's Sons, New York, 1964.

Kahn v. Shevin, 42 United States Law Week 4591 (1974).

Korematsu v. United States, 232 United States Reports 214 (1944).

"The Law and the Lady—Some Who Practice the Profession and Their Success," 60 *Albany Law Journal* 91 (1899).

Lerner, Gerda: *The Woman in American History,* Addison-Wesley Co. Publishing Company, Inc., Reading, Mass., 1971.

Lerner, Gerda: "So You Think You Know Women's History," *Ms.,* p. 32, September 1972.

Muller v. Oregon, 208 United States Reports 412 (1908).

"Note—Death of Mrs. Myra Bradwell," 28 *American Law Review* 278 (1894).

"Note—Myra Bradwell," 3 *Michigan Law Journal* 77 (1894).

Pettus, Isabella M.: "The Legal Education of Women," 61 *Albany Law Journal* 325 (1900).

Reed v. Reed, 404 United States Reports 71 (1972).

Reed v. State, 123 Texas Criminal Reports 348 (1933).

Roe v. Wade, 410 United States Reports 113 (1973).

Sail'er Inn, Inc. v. Kirby, 5 California Reports 3d 1 (1971).

Smith, Elizabeth: "Letter from Med. School Sister," *Sister,* vol. 4, no. 5, p. 5, July 1973.

Stevens, Robert: "Two Cheers for 1870: The American Law School," in Donald Fleming and Bernard Bailyn (eds.), *Perspectives in American History,* vol. 5, Charles Warren Center for Studies in American History, Harvard University, Cambridge, Mass., 1971.

Tocqueville, Alexis de: *Democracy in America,* vol. 1, Phillips Bradley (trans.), Vintage Books, New York, 1956.

Trebilcock, Anne: "Women in Law," *Women's Studies Newsletter,* no. 5, p. 2, Fall 1973.

Van Alstyne, William: "A Comment on Preferential Hiring by Race or Sex, and the Position of the American Civil Liberties Union," American Civil Liberties Union, New York, Jan. 26, 1973.

Wallach, Aleta: "Genesis of a 'Women and the Law' Course: The Dawn of Consciousness at UCLA Law School," 24 *Journal of Legal Education* 309 (1972).

Wallach, Aleta: "Women's Studies in the Law School," in Nancy Hoffman, Cynthia Secor, and Adrian Tinsley (eds.), *Female Studies VI, Closer to the Ground, Women's Classes, Criticism, Programs— 1972,* The Feminist Press, Old Westbury, N.Y., 1972.

Warren, Charles: *A History of the American Bar,* Little, Brown and Company, Boston, 1911.

4. Women and the Power to Change

by Florence Howe

In the summer of 1964, when Northern activists arrived in
Jackson, Mississippi, we found there an organization called
Womanpower Unlimited. Founded by Clarie Collins Harvey, a
black businesswoman and church leader, Womanpower surprised me, not because it was an organization of women, but
because it was integrated. Black women and white had come
together to change racial relationships in their community.
Meetings were relatively open in Jackson, but private elsewhere
in the state. Several Northern white women accompanied Ms.
Harvey to the Gulf Coast on the occasion of one meeting, secret
even from the husbands of women attending. A first experience
in social integration for these women, the meeting's ambience
was memorable: the triumph of achieving an unauthorized
meeting; the anticipation of whether and how to go "public" and
what might be achieved thereby; the excitement of discovering
that, despite the racial lines, women had mutual concerns about
their children's education and the general welfare of their
communities.

No one talked more coherently about the "power" of women
than Ms. Harvey, though without any threat to male dominance.
While black women could be natural leaders, as her behavior
demonstrated, they drew power from their inferior status.
Women were less visible than men; therefore more movement
was possible for them. Even if their private meetings had been
discovered, as they had been in Jackson, what could it matter
that some black and white women were talking together? A few
husbands might be irritated, but women's meetings suggested
no threat to the principled segregation of the community that a
parallel meeting among their husbands might have signified.
Nor could it evoke the kinds of sensationalized fears that

127

meetings among younger women and men of both races had provoked that hot Mississippi summer. The strategy was designed to accomplish change slowly and without provoking fear, hostility, or confrontation: it relied upon patriarchy. After all, what could a few women do? Charity was their line and had been for decades. Charity—not change. Yet of course, these were women using their "womanpower" for change.

I begin with this isolated instance of a decade ago in part because I can think of no other recent instance in which the word "power" has been publicly used by a group of women either to name an organization or to promote one.[1] Indeed, I can cite one instance less than five years ago in which the word was deliberately avoided. After the first public meeting of the Professional Women's Caucus, a small but representative group assembled to discuss, among other things, a new name for the organization. One possibility offering the acronym of "POWER" was immediately and utterly rejected. Discussion was hardly necessary, except to explain how unsuitable a term "power" was, especially for professional women who, by virtue of their status, had more power than most other women.

By the late sixties, black power and student power were part of the common parlance. Why *not* woman power? Interestingly, those suggesting the acronym were among the group's conservative, prestigious, and nonacademic members. But they were new to the women's movement, and they had not caught the pulse of its grass roots energy, where the word "power" was to be avoided at all costs, though the principle slogan was "sisterhood is powerful." It is important to understand why POWER alone as slogan and ruling concept has consistently been anathema to a women's movement interested not as much in its relationship to the outside male world as in its ability to organize other women.

In one sense the explanation is remarkably simple: the word power suggests control of one group by another, and hence, its

---

[1] While there are still no signs of the organizational use of the term, I expect that "power" will become, in the next year, a subject of some fresh theoretical concern to feminists. The Modern Language Association's Commission on the Status of Women decided, in February 1974, to plan a forum on the subject Women, Literature, and Power for the 1974 December Convention of the association. At least two writers, Elizabeth Janeway and John McClusky, plan books on aspects of women and power.

use by a subordinate group may evoke in the dominant one a fear of insurrection. The letters of Abigail Adams and John Adams illustrate that notion amusingly. In March 1776, Abigail wrote to her husband John, who was beginning to write the laws of a new government:

Remember the Ladies, and be more generous and favourable to them than your ancestors. Do not put such unlimited power into the hands of the Husbands. Remember all men would be tyrants if they could. If perticuliar [*sic*] care and attention is not paid to the Laidies [*sic*], we are determined to foment a Rebellion, and will not hold ourselves bound by any Laws in which we have no voice, or Representation (Rossi, 1973, pp. 10–11).

John responded two weeks later,

Depend upon it, we know better than to repeal our Masculine systems. Altho they are in full Force, you know they are little more than Theory. We dare not exert our Power in its full Latitude. We are obliged to go fair, and softly, and in Practice you know We are the subjects. We have only the Name of Masters, and rather than give up this, which would compleatly subject Us to the Despotism of the Peticoat, I hope General Washington, and all our brave Heroes would fight (ibid., p. 11).

While invoking an insurrection of "peticoats" suggests Pope's delicate satire on women's foibles written 50 years earlier, it also lays out the ideology of patriarchy, even with some of its complexity. The "Masculine system" is named, but it is alleged to be merely a theory: "in Practice," women are so powerful that only the "Name of Masters" allows men any power at all. While this is obviously the wildest exaggeration, it is formed on the basis of commonly held assumptions: male power is allegedly controlled by hidden, female power (wives, secretaries, assistants, even mothers); if men were to lose the facade of power, they would have nothing else. Obviously again exaggerated, even this kind of logic excludes at least three other possibilities: first, that men might themselves try the use of secret (husband, male secretary or assistant, even father) power over women; or second, that power might be shared; or third, that power might *not* be conceived as a finite commodity through which one person or group controls another, either secretly or openly.

But the issue of women and power has generally been raised in a framework that insists upon a competitive struggle with men.

Rousseau, for example, put the problem into one sentence: "Educate women like men," he said, "and the more they resemble our sex the less power will they have over us" (Wollstonecraft, 1967, p. 107). Behind this sentence lie several complex assumptions: education is directly related to power; the education of women and men, like the power of each in relation to the other, must be distinctive and distinctly related to the patriarchy in which they exist. The sentence also suggests the possibility that education might undo what Rousseau and others of his time (and since) believed were innate differences accounting for man's superior and woman's inferior abilities and achievements. Mary Wollstonecraft's answer to Rousseau significantly directs the woman's movement even to this day. It is a delightfully simple response: "I do not want them [women] to have power over men," she wrote, "but over themselves" (Wollstonecraft, 1967, p. 107). Margaret Fuller, writing more than 50 years later, made almost the identical point: "Were they free, were they wise fully to develop the strength and beauty of Woman; they would never wish to be men, or man-like . . ." (Fuller, 1971, p. 63).

In one sense, Wollstonecraft and Fuller mean to be reassuring to men: we don't want your turf or your power; we simply want a room of our own, a space in which we can develop our potential, whatever that may be. Nineteenth-century feminists were modest enough about possibilities, admitting openly to man's greater physical strength, for example, and suggesting that it was impossible to "prove" whether or not women's intellectual capacity was precisely equivalent to men's. On the other hand, it was clear enough that whatever the potential of women, their education and their inequality before the law, to take only two elements, contributed significantly to their inferior status. What nineteenth-century feminists asked for, therefore, was equality before the law, and even more difficult to achieve, equality in the human consciousness that would allow women to develop whatever capacities they might have.

But things are never as simple as they seem. To insist that a woman wished to control her own life—and, in the twentieth century, her own body—may, on the surface, seem to be nonthreatening to men. To demand equality for women even in the nineteenth century was to insist that laws be changed, for example, or that colleges be opened to women. To suggest that such change would not also affect men's lives was either naïve or tactful. Obviously, I believe that the movement has not only attempted to be tactful; it has also tended to operate within the boundaries created by its own state of oppression. That oppression has taught women certain techniques for survival, among them the idea of cultivating their own garden, without infringing on male territory. To a significant extent, this has been the history of women through the past two centuries of struggle.

Even the 70-year battle for suffrage was not, in itself, an infringement on male territory, though it was certainly fought as an infringement on a male prerogative. For suffrage was not linked to officeholding, or to sharing the power for decision making at the legislative, executive, and judicial levels of government.[2] Thus, allowing women the right to vote was allowing them to vote for this man or that one, exactly as men in the society did. Similarly, admitting women to higher education did not alter the power relationships between women and men: women either filled subordinate slots in the hierarchy or filled entire ghettos of professional life, the elementary school, for example, or nursing and social work. Even in totally woman-dominated academic and professional areas, male power has consistently been at the top.

It is not surprising, therefore, that men assume that women might want power in order to move "up" and replace them, or that "giving" women power would in effect reduce the power of men. Indeed, the view is based on the traditional concept of power as a finite quantity of control that one person or group exercises over another person or group. If a husband has power, theoretically a wife does not; if the leader of a group is powerful, theoretically the members of that group must be without power. It's a view of power as commodity: they who control the oil reserves have it, or he who owns the factory. Such a conception of power extends itself deeply into the society and hence into the thinking of its members: some one person or group *must be* better, stronger, smarter, more beautiful than the rest. An anecdote may illustrate this kind of thinking.

---

[2] It is also true that granting suffrage to women when they did helped preserve the power of established males over challengers to that establishment—like workers.

In 1967, at a community meeting in Washington, D.C., a small group of middle-class white mothers of a tiny minority of children attending an elementary school in a relatively poor black neighborhood were protesting the addition of new texts focused on the lives of black children. "If you teach these children to be proud of the fact that they're black," one white mother cried out *in extremis,* "where will that leave my children?" When several black mothers, in their astonishment protested, and others wept openly, and still others walked out, the white women could not understand or believe that they were responsible for the despair and disillusion that followed—or the anger. From their point of view, at least in 1967, if black were to be beautiful, clever, strong, then white must become ugly, stupid, weak.

In 1974, the terms are replaceable by male and female. I have heard mothers and female elementary school teachers say that if you "raise girls' self-esteem," you will necessarily "threaten the boys'." Again, the assumptions are drawn from the traditional view of power as a finite commodity that some, and not others, possess. According to that view, power becomes the object of a struggle to gain and hold superiority: the fulcrum can never be truly in balance. Indeed, a change of power in this sense—as we have heard people say time and again—changes nothing really, since power, the exercise by one group of control over others' lives, continues under a different face.

It is not surprising also, therefore, that inside the women's movement, probably only one word has carried more negative affect than "power," and that word has been "male." Indeed, the two words have tended for obvious reasons to become synonymous. Male power, private or institutionalized, has traditionally controlled most aspects of the lives of women, whatever their color or class, not only through the rule of law and coercion, but more subtly through the promise of love or the threat of its loss. John Stuart Mill, more than a century ago, wrote movingly about the power of husbands over wives:

Whatever gratification of pride there is in the possession of power, and whatever personal interest in its exercise, is in this case not confined to a limited class, but common to the whole male sex. . . . it comes home to the person and hearth of every male head of a family, and of every one who looks forward to being so. The clodhopper exercises, or is to exercise, his share of the power equally with the highest nobleman. . . . In the case of women, each individual of the subject-class is in a chronic state of bribery and intimidation combined.

. . . Men do not want solely the obedience of women, they want their sentiments. All men, except the most brutish, desire to have, in the woman most nearly connected with them, not a forced slave but a willing one, not a slave merely, but a favourite. They have therefore put everything in practice to enslave their minds. . . . When we put together three things—first, the natural attraction between opposite sexes; secondly, the wife's entire dependence on the husband, every privilege or pleasure she has being either his gift, or depending entirely on his will; and lastly, that the principal object of human pursuit, consideration, and all objects of social ambition, can in general be sought or obtained by her only through him, it would be a miracle if the object of being attractive to men had not become the polar star of feminine education and formation of character. And, this great means of influence over the minds of women having been acquired, an instinct of selfishness made men avail themselves of it to the utmost as a means of holding women in subjection, by representing to them meekness, submissiveness, and resignation of all individual will into the hands of a man, as an essential part of sexual attractiveness (Rossi, 1973, pp. 136, 141).

Mill's view is important for its emphasis on what we now call socialization: the use of power to effect *internal* acceptance of external authority. As a result of the power of men, women have learned to believe in their own inferiority; indeed, as mothers and teachers of the young, women become instruments of "male" power.

The problems for women who understand the male use of traditional power are complex: How to break away from a force so all-encompassing? How to do so without assuming its guise and thus reversing patriarchal relationships and simply substituting females for the men in charge of institutions? In other words, how to change the power that controls women's lives without extending oppression either to other women, to groups of minorities, or to men themselves. In this essay, I want to answer those questions especially as they relate to academic women and the institutions in which they work. I am especially interested both in the manner in which teachers exercise their authority in the classroom and in the ways in which groups of teachers might begin to work together to change the education of women and men. In the next section I shall explore an alternative concept of power that has developed within the women's movement.

WOMEN'S POWER: A LIBERATING FORCE FOR CHANGE Conventionally conceived, power is the control exercised by one person or group over others. Whether the controlling person is a husband, a political leader, a school principal, a department chairman, or a classroom teacher, the exercise of power is typically elitist, hierarchical, authoritarian, and manipulatively dependent on reward and punishment. Whether the powerless are wives, citizens, teachers, or students, the exercise of power thrives both on their fears and on their acceptance, through socialization as well as through more direct means of control, of their permanent subjection. Obviously, such power is debilitating to those under its sway. Obviously also, power thus conceived has been identified as "male."

The expression, "the power of women," conjures up something different: witchcraft, for example, including conception and childbirth, thought to be original "powers" of women, mysterious in origin and frightening in practice. The power of women's beauty to inspire male genius is a commonplace of literature and the other arts. The power of women's virtue, especially her virginity, was enough to inspire the gods. With the possible exception of witchery, these were powers rooted in female biology; they were also transient. Most important, they functioned only in relation to individual men (or gods)—not with respect to the organization of society. Obviously, the powers of female beauty, witchery, pregnancy, and chastity, confined to women as they are, could not substitute for legal or political power. Indeed, offered as substitutes in a society that values legal and political power—as well as money, work, accomplishment, position—they become a means to keep women powerless.

Whatever the conceptions of women's power, in reality it has been covert and private: an exercise in cunning and winsome guile, practiced on allegedly unsuspecting husbands, lovers, fathers, brothers, sons. As Rousseau describes it, "A woman who is naturally weak, and does not carry her ideas to any great extent, knows how to judge and make a proper estimate of those movements which she sets to work, in order to aid her weakness; and those movements are the passions of men." Rousseau prescribes for a woman's education the thorough "study" of "the dispositions of those men to whom she is subject." Like John Adams who wrote after him, Rousseau also attempts to disparage the powers of male supremacy: "The mechanism she employs," he says, writing chiefly but not only of a woman's ability to provoke men's sexuality, "is much more powerful than ours; for all her levers move the human heart." Powerful or not, women's chief role and purpose in life was to please men. As Rousseau describes the education of women, it is consistently "relative to the men":

To please, to be useful to us, to make us love and esteem them, to educate us when young, and take care of us when grown up, to advise, to console us, to render our lives easy and agreeable—these are the duties of women at all times, and what they should be taught in their infancy (in Wollstonecraft, 1967, pp. 76, 131).

Thus woman's "power" is confined to her private life and her education prescribed to maintain her ability to "please" that man to whom she owes her status as wife.

The power of women as a force for change in the nineteenth century was built on their perception of themselves as individually powerless: to change that condition, they adopted strategies they had learned in the abolitionist movement and in other contemporary movements for change, including that of moral reform and temperance. Essentially, they organized masses of women into large national organizations capable of accumulating millions of signatures on a petition, turning out thousands of marchers in a demonstration, or writing countless letters to Congress. They built their movement not on public denunciations of men, though they expressed their disappointments on that count privately in correspondence, but on the "rights" of women, even as announced officially in the 1848 "Declaration of Sentiments." The nineteenth-century movement built on the vision of a righteous and energized population of women—half the nation—strong in their conviction that they deserved "equality" before the law and in the minds of men. The 70-year struggle to convince men of women's right to vote is evidence of both the determination of women and the reluctance of men to change the nation's legal patriarchy.

Like its nineteenth-century counterpart, the contemporary women's movement began with a concept of mass organizing of women to gain legal rights, not to suffrage, but primarily to equity in employment and salary scales. A second strand of the movement, begun almost simultaneously, grew out of the civil rights and antiwar movements. These women did not attempt national organization, but focused on building networks of small consciousness-raising groups in particular cities. They also attempted a number of visible "actions," one of which gained for women's liberation the indelible label of "bra-burners."[3] By 1969, the slogan "sisterhood is powerful" dominated both segments of the women's movement and expressed its main direction: to organize women around issues that connected rather than divided them: birth control and abortion; child care; education; work. Such groups as the National Organization of Women (NOW, founded in 1966) aimed to gather numbers of women as a potent pressure for change on many issues. The Women's Equity Action League (WEAL, founded in 1968) focused both its membership and its concerns on bringing class action suits against higher education for its treatment of women. The dominant mode through which organizing was eventually accomplished both for the large national organizations and for the radical feminist groups was the small consciousness-raising group.

"The concept of 'consciousness-raising,'" according to Juliet Mitchell, "is the reinterpretation of a Chinese revolutionary practice of 'speaking bitterness'. . . . Like Chinese peasants who took a step out of thinking their fate was natural by describing the conditions of their lives to each other, middle-class women in the U.S. brought the facts of their own lives to the surface."[4] "The first symptom of oppression is the repression

---

[3] I am sorry to say that there never was a bra-burning, but rather the symbolic disposal of such items and others in a trash can before the 1968 Atlantic City beauty pageant. These and other memorable events have now been chronicled at length in the first of several books on the new women's movement (see Carden, 1974).

[4] I don't suppose that most women who have been in consciousness-raising groups are necessarily aware of their analogy to Chinese forms. Obviously, there were several elements in the United States culture that allowed for the spread of such groups: the coffee klatch, for example, the quilting bee, and other forms of female social or work groups made the idea of discussion sessions quite natural, though the "rules" for consciousness-raising groups set them apart from such precedents. It is also true that in a society that places value on psychotherapy, such groups were seen as having potential therapeutic value, as indeed they do. In the Southern civil rights movement, discussion groups, especially on the subject of racism, also provided a precedent.

of words," Mitchell writes; "the state of suffering is so total and so assumed that it is not known to be there." "Speaking bitterness" brings to consciousness the barely conscious; when the process occurs publicly, in a small group, "one person's realization of an injustice brings to mind other injustices for the whole group" (Mitchell, 1971, p. 62). Both in China and in the United States, the process is part of an educational strategy.

In the United States consciousness-raising groups turned the women's movement into a teaching movement that was functionally both massive and yet totally decentralized—even into tiny splinters. Spread across the nation, the process was codified not only for the purpose of raising the consciousness of women about their relations with men, but also as a means of establishing new relationships among women. To be "sisterly" rather than competitive and backbiting was not only personal but political, since cooperation and supportive behavior enabled otherwise powerless women to work together toward change. One did not simply "make friends" with women; one became political "sisters" in a growing women's movement.

That movement openly eschewed "male power" in all its forms. In their place, women substituted the allegedly leaderless group. Theoretically, if no one person was "in charge" of a consciousness-raising group, then all were "equally" in charge. In practice, at least one person in the group probably had had experience enough to inform others of the "rules." In practice also, of course, all groups develop their own leadership, though the structure may remain covert. The rules called for an atmosphere of loving and supportive acceptance of all women in the group, whatever their experiences, ideas, values, or problems. Direct criticisms of or challenges to another woman's statement were not acceptable "sisterly" behavior, nor were dependence on outside authorities, deference to a woman's particular "status," or domination of the group by any one or more persons. One technique widely adopted attempted to encourage both the shy to speak and the bold to speak briefly: on an agreed-upon question, experience, or topic, each person in the group would speak in succession, with no fear either of interruptions or of cross-examination or debate-like challenges. Thus, a group of twelve might spend more than an hour—each of them in turn—describing an early sexual encounter or last week's most unpleasant sexist experience. The circle completed, one person might attempt a sisterly comment or question: "Alice, what you said was very moving. How would you handle the same experience today?" And Alice's response might make a connection to Laura's experience, or perhaps she or Laura might ask others how they would look at such an experience today. The process is not a showy one—there are few or no flashes of brilliant strategy; the gestures tend to be quiet, sharing ones that open the talk to those who are unaccustomed to speaking their thoughts out loud.

From the talk and the sharing come discoveries familiar to social science: alleged personal deviance is, in fact, social reality. Guilt about wifely or motherly boredom, desires for a working life or an education previously denied are common to middle-class women, not because they are personally maladjusted but because they were socialized to accept their insufficient social roles. The second stage in the educational process occurs when some member of the group takes the leap from consciousness to action. She might ask a husband or a lover, for example, to share some aspect of housework or child care, and if successful she might thus learn that it is possible to alter the pattern of her life. Successful, too, she becomes a "model" of encouragement for others in the group. When this leap occurs, the consciousness-raising group becomes a "support" group for women who are in the process of changing their personal lives and becoming thus at least part of a women's movement engaged in similar efforts.

It is easy to underestimate the importance of these consciousness-raising groups. They are open to various criticisms and have felt them from those both inside and outside the movement. For one thing, feminists have been concerned lest the illusion of "leaderless" groups perpetuate systematic manipulation within the movement, as well as a continued ignorance about the nature of power and leadership. For another, the groups have seemed, both in their singular introversion and in their isolation from each other, relatively unimportant, and hardly "political." Originally conceived, groups were thought to be capable of educating women whose raised consciousness would give them the power not only to change their personal lives but to join forces as part of a movement to change institutions in their communities. For many complex reasons, consciousness-raising groups succeeded only for a relatively short period in building networks for activist projects in major cities. Most of these networks—in Boston, New York, Chicago, and Washington,

D.C., for example—are now dead, their members either out of the organized movement, or more likely, swelling the membership of NOW, WEAL, and the National Women's Political Caucus.

Politically, the consciousness-raising groups are very important, especially if one wishes to understand an alternative concept of power promulgated by the movement. The emphasis on "sisterhood," despite additional consciousness about class and race differences, allows the movement to function as a "mass." It allows trade union women to feel a sense of "solidarity" with college professors (now increasingly, of course, joining those labor ranks). And so, despite the isolation of individual groups in particular communities, the message is one of importance for national movement building, because it allows for precisely what the nineteenth-century movement accomplished though its emphasis on the "rights" of women. While the traditionally powerful assert the possession of power as a commodity, to be exchanged for other commodities like money, approval, service, and time, and organize the acquisition of power though competition, an alternative view, built on sisterhood, makes an effort to diffuse power.[5]

Power diffused in the group, and even into many thousands of groups, of course, is not to be confused with the power to make significant changes in institutions. The chief contribution of the consciousness-raising group continues to be an educational one: women learn not only about the sexual politics of their own lives but about the power potentially present in "sisterhood." The large step, from controlling one's own life to working with others on some ultimate political goal, is, of course, not an automatic one, though I think it would be fair to state that even if the consciousness-raising group does not motivate women to work actively in the movement per se, it often sends them into the

---

[5] I am obliged to Paul Lauter for adding this conceptualization when he read this manuscript in draft. He added: "The effort of the powerless, by contrast, is to diffuse power and, I begin to think, break its connections with commodities. A central question: can you 'buy' power—that is, exchange money for it? If you can, you can also exchange power *for* money, and therefore for privilege and all the other commodities, which is what the Chinese mean by the 'capitalist road' in the Soviet Union. The 'socialist road' of the cultural revolution leads toward that equal diffusion of power among all *and* toward breaking the commodity tie (power/money) so that leadership and authority are no longer the paths to elitism, possession, privatization of power."

work force or back to college, where they may also encounter the movement in the form, for example, of trade union caucuses or women's studies programs.

Most women in the movement on campus and off have had the experience of consciousness-raising groups. They bring a new ambience to committee work, to leadership, and to political organizing generally. The variety of power exercised by such women is neither covert power in Rousseau's sense, nor the traditional, authoritarian form of "male" power previously described. Despite the media's image-making effect, the tone of rank-and-file feminist leadership is low-key but firm. In male circles, its openness may, indeed, be disarming. I have seen women, for example, move formally that the chair request that all persons on a committee successively state their views openly on a particular matter; and I have seen that request become an established pattern in the group.

The practice of feminist leadership is, of course, of special significance if one believes that leaders set the tone of groups by acting as role models for others. That is, authoritarian leaders may build authoritarian followers, so that up and down the line of hierarchy there is no possibility of an interchange between subjects and rulers, leaders and followers. Or leaders may be, as in the case of the charismatic Martin Luther King, Jr., symbolic or strategic role models for followers who are neither subject to him nor in his "control."[6] The experience of "leaderless" groups convinced many feminists of the need for open and democratically shared authority, and especially for *public* decision making. When leadership is covert, its control depends on additional meetings (or telephone calls) outside the established ones, and it is possible therefore for certain members, systematically excluded from such relationships, to be controlled, even as in the traditional manner of patriarchy. Knowledgeable feminists will insist, therefore, on democratic procedures for establishing leadership, and either on the systematic rotation of that power or on

---

[6] Quite by accident, I met Iowa political scientist John McClusky in January 1974 at a work conference on educational leadership, where we were assigned to the same writing team. We produced a paper called "Hierarchy, Power, and Women in Educational Policy Making," to be published shortly. McClusky's doctoral dissertation, focused on conceptualizations of "liberating" as distinct from "debilitating" forms of power, describes the political career of Martin Luther King in detail. McClusky's unpublished papers are available from him.

procedures for ensuring decentralization. Feminist groups may function entirely through a committee structure that depends upon one or two "coordinators" to convene the group for decision making.

While an open system of decision making is important, it is also dependent upon maintaining the broadest possible "base" of *informed* support. Perhaps the single most important lesson that feminists have learned both from critiques of the male establishment (including the male *left* establishment) and from the manipulative exercise of power by covert feminist leadership is the need for sharing information. Thus, in the first few years of its existence, in what was appropriately called the "mushroom effect," the women's movement spawned some 2,000 publications, many of them newsletters published by local consortia of consciousness-raising groups or by chapters of NOW. In addition, most feminist organizations or groups I am acquainted with, including women's studies programs, also publish, for a broad constituency that typically extends beyond its immediate participants, elaborate "minutes" of meetings or monthly or annual reports of their accomplishments and goals. These efforts make manifest the continual importance of building a broad-based movement, for while consciousness and knowledge are not to be confused with power, they are both essential to its exercise.

I am not of the feminist school that believes in the moral superiority of women or in the superiority of any group of people. Nor do I believe that women possess any special "power" or capacity.[7] But I do believe that it is possible for a group of people who have been historically subjected to adverse conditions and treatment to develop alternative cultural forms of survival and political strategies for change. The consciousness-raising group and open forms of leadership and information sharing are two important political developments. During the past five years, these have become influential on campuses, especially where women's studies programs have functioned as

---

[7] Aside from the biological capacity to conceive and bear children, that is. All people are born with capacities or "powers" that the world they live in may encourage or deny. Despite many efforts of researchers, there has still been no hard evidence that distinguishes between the innate capacities of humans by sex or race.

the academic arm of the women's movement. But a viable political strategy depends on numbers, on large organizations, and on long-range planning. For the kind of change to occur that feminists envision—not simply replacing a male authority figure in or out of the classroom with a female one—women need both patience and persistence. Since feminists are interested in changing not only the concept of power as a finite commodity but the manner in which power is exercised, the process of such change becomes important.

In the next section, I shall trace the process of such change for one academic woman who did not join the movement until the movement reached the campus—in 1969. While I was involved in other movements before 1969, it is fair to say that the women's movement changed the direction of my life, indeed gave my life the meaning it had not theretofore had.

THE DECLINE OF POWERLESS- NESS

A little more than ten years ago, several students introduced me to political activism through an innocent enough request for a lift from their suburban campus to the city where a picket line was in progress at a segregated movie theater. Instead of dropping them off, I joined the picket line, and, in a manner familiar enough to those academics who have survived their activism, became a "campus radical" at a rather conservative women's college. My reputation changed slowly during the course of the next several years, in part because I attempted, with relatively little con- sciousness about the effort, to continue my old style of life even while donning the new. I cannot now remember the context, but I do remember one day on which I knew that something had changed for me forever, and it is from that time that I chart the decline of my powerlessness. A male colleague, observing my unhappy expression through a lengthy interchange with two other male colleagues, commented afterward, "You can't please people and be 'political' at the same time. Some people are bound to disagree with you; you're going to offend others; and you'll have to get used to being disliked—or give in."

I was, of course, defensive: I didn't *need* to please people, I protested. But the conversation in the narrow hall outside our offices flags my earliest consciousness of how sharp the contrast was between my need to please not only superiors but peers and my growing commitment to self-determination and activism. The theme is typical enough for women, academics or not: we are socialized in a manner quite distinct from males, so that we develop a need for "affiliation," not "achievement."[8] What a woman might want to do or to learn is second to another critical question: what is it desirable that she do or learn? The process of socialization leads to a feeling of powerlessness, or, more precisely, pleasing others expresses the powerlessness of women in our culture. Women learn to measure themselves against others' standards or needs—parents', teachers', husband's, or lover's—registering value in their eyes. I took my cues especially from teachers; ironically, it was in discovering a different role for myself as teacher that the decline of my powerlessness began.

Toward the end of my sophomore year at college, I switched from science to English without so much as regret, much less anger, about the two years spent on human physiology, mathematics, "scientific" German, and chemistry. During that semester, my mathematics teacher called me into her office. She was puzzled, she said, about two errors I had made on a recent near-perfect examination. It was not, she assured me, that she was questioning my honesty, for all my grades had been excellent; rather, she was curious about my reasoning: in one problem, I had chosen a unique method of solution. A skilled teacher, she quickly discovered that no "creative" mathematical mind had been at work: I had simply chosen the wrong equation. She discovered, on further questioning, that while my study habits assured an ability to memorize equations, and even to choose them accurately for application, I could not, in words, describe their theories or functions. At about the same time, my chemistry teacher, mystified by A's in organic and C's in inorganic, also saw me in conference. Both teachers separately urged me to leave science, and without further ado or discussion, I did.

Discrimination? In the ordinary sense, I should have to dismiss that charge, for this was Hunter College in the late forties, when all the students and most of the faculty were women, and when there were, of course, many women science majors. But what these two women were saying to me was that women had

---

[8] These psychological terms have become commonplace in the academic women's movement, especially following the work of Matina Horner (1969) on the "achievement theory" of McClelland and others (1953). For a brief summary, see Chapter 10 of Judith M. Bardwick's *Psychology of Women* (1971).

to be not simply good or mediocre in science, but excellent; and that a female who had grown up afraid of mathematics and science, and who was hence somewhat backward conceptually, could not be reeducated, not even at the age of 18.

And I, at 18, accepted their diagnosis as I would the reading of an x-ray machine: no tears, no anger marked the scene for me. I would be an English teacher and not a science teacher. What mattered was becoming a teacher and so fulfilling my mother's own thwarted ambition. From the day I entered kindergarten, the idea was fixed in my head that I would become, some day, that teacher at the head of the room. Part of the curriculum for me each year was studying how to become "teacher."

I might never have had that two-year interlude in science had it not been for a high school English teacher who told me, confidentially, after long hours of work on the Hunter High School literary magazine one day, that I was one of the students she most liked working with. I was, she continued, the ideal "good" student, one who could write straightforward prose, but who had not a "creative" bone in her body. I believed that teacher, accepted her diagnosis again without a pang or murmur. She was the teacher; she knew. And I crossed English off my list.[9]

I do not think I am exceptional in this matter, but my class background contributed additional fears and feelings of inadequacy to the ordinary female socialization. Until I left Brooklyn's Jewish ghetto for Hunter College High School, I had had no difficulty making my way, for I was bright and hardworking, and exceptionally sensitive to satisfying other people's desires or needs, especially teachers'. At Hunter High, however, I didn't speak for one entire year, and my academic record was only mildly above mediocrity. The first teacher to hear my diction sent me to a speech "therapist" who pronounced me "defective," handed me a small mirror, and assigned me to special after-school classes to rid me of dentalization, nasality, and other venial crimes. In that year, I wiped out my Brooklyn working-

---

[9] By the time I returned to English, I had learned that one did not need to *be* creative. But I had taken this teacher's judgment so to heart that, when at college I had been selected, on the basis of my work in freshman composition, for a creative writing class, I petitioned to avoid it and to do the regular critical writing course instead.

class accent, but I never again spoke freely in a classroom until, at the University of Wisconsin, I became a teaching assistant.

Thus, in choosing my major, my speech, even my "career," I looked outward to satisfy others' demands upon me. My mother set the goal, and my teachers became the rods against which I measured the possibility for accomplishing that goal. Pleasing others reflected an approach to schooling and to study that began with decisions and standards not my own. When a professor suggested that I was "good at ideas" and offered me a thesis subject, I slavishly followed his suggestion, grateful that it saved me the trouble of finding one for myself. It was not that I was entirely uncritical of teachers; rather, the teacher who influenced me became, in each case, my unquestioned authority.

As a novice instructor, I taught in a style I had grown accustomed to seeing as a student. I was a direct, clear, organized, and controlling teacher who told students what she wanted and who expected to be pleased by their doing as they were told. Most of my teaching at Wisconsin lent itself well enough to that scheme, since freshman composition was the funnel through which all high school graduates had to pass in order to remain at the universities.[10] In that class, I taught a standardized curriculum of grammar, punctuation, sentence style, and prose organization, designed to train competent essay writers of the style that Hunter College High School had defined for me. The essays these students produced were utterly unrelated to their racial, class, or ethnic origins, or to whether they were male or female. I was interested only in turning out people, who, like myself, had learned to bury even their local accents, to become that middle-American male voice that one hears on news broadcasts and reads in weekly news magazines. As I reconsider my training—and thinking—I feel most astounded by this particular failure: to assume that one can teach writing without understanding that feelings and thoughts arise out of particular personal and social conditions. And it helps me to comprehend why I was not a particularly astute or confident critic of literature, and why, as a graduate student, I was careful

---

[10] In those days before universities' "tracking" systems, a form of open admissions prevailed. Freshman English was one of the hurdles designed to thin the entering population, and teaching assistants were unwitting accomplices to the "cooling-out" system (see Clark, 1960).

to choose only "straight research" topics, never "creative" or evaluative ones.

Literature as I had studied it and as I later began to teach it was a "subject"—to be learned as I had learned formulas. It was also to be worshipped as the best that had ever been thought and written down, as a kind of religion *cum* philosophy, a substitute for moral guidance and for "universals" about the major "facts" of life, which, as I reflect upon them, were mostly suffering and death. Thus, Andromache's pain at the loss of Hector was every woman's pain at the death of a husband killed at war. And Hamlet's heroic efforts, excesses, and suffering were the model for those who would expose and punish sin and corruption. While this is not an impossible reading of literature, it is not especially helpful for students who would learn to write it or even to read it with some independent judgment of its values or portrayals of life. Nor is it a reading of literature that is particularly interesting or thought-provoking, since it asks no questions, sets no problems. It is conventionally moralistic and assumes that all can agree on "rational values" and that all readers are one reader. Most important, it sets up the teacher as authority on the meaning of literature.

That I read and taught literature in this fashion is not surprising, since I had spent more than two decades of a lifetime denying my own identity. I was a Jew and had avoided both the language of my childhood as well as its literature and culture. As an American immigrant's granddaughter, I had painfully learned proper voice, diction, and syntax, as well as a "correct" prose style, but I had avoided American literature and culture, prefer-ring British medieval, renaissance, and eighteenth-century liter-ature and history. I was a woman of working-class origins, but it never occurred to me to inquire whether women or working-class people generally had produced literature. In short, I chose to study literature distant from me in time and space and read, as Elaine Showalter has suggested that most women do, as an anthropologist investigating a strange (male) culture (Showalter, 1971).

By 1960, I had become so much a part of that male culture that I sneered openly at the idea of teaching on a women's campus. But my interest in teaching made me accept a temporary one-year appointment at Goucher College. As I had at Smith (where I had earned a master's degree), I worried about my clothes, my lack of "good" jewelry, family name, and academic connections. I still could not play tennis or ride a horse, and it was becoming increasingly difficult for me to admit, much less explain, those lapses. The snob in me won out. I was cold and aloof as a teacher. Students described me as "formidable." My behavior, of course, was also precisely what was expected by peers and superiors on the faculty and in the administration. There I became a most pleasant "daughter," especially to the male faculty a decade or so older than I, and to the dean. When it was clear that I was to stay on campus at least for another year, I was assigned the responsibility (with a young male teacher) of redesigning the required sophomore course for English majors. With utter disregard for our women students, we chose a series of "major" and "universal" works—from *Dr. Faustus* and *Paradise Lost,* through *The Prelude* and a half dozen others, to *The Waste Land*—in which there appeared not a single woman author nor a single admirable woman as central character.[11] I stayed at Goucher to teach that and other male-centered courses for nearly half a decade, and I might have continued to act the misogynist English teacher had I not volunteered, in the summer of 1964, to teach in the Mississippi Freedom Schools.

I arrived in Mississippi nervous to the point of anxiety and yet eager for my work to begin. I was nervous because I had expected to teach black history and literature, and although I had been cramming, I was not even a novice in those areas. Nevertheless, I wanted to begin at once. Much to my dismay, there was a weekend of "orientation," aimed mainly at keeping the summer volunteers alive through teaching them rules for survival, as well as procedures to follow if harassed or arrested. Another two days of meetings followed, in which I began to act as a rapid-talking, impatient know-it-all Northerner, who wanted to cut through the seemingly aimless talk and get to the work of teaching. I remember being taken aside by Tom Wahman and Staughton Lynd, codirectors of the Freedom Schools, and asked, kindly but firmly, to abstain from speaking for the afternoon, and instead to listen to local black people and some younger black and white students try to work things out for

---

[11] Indeed, the only admirable female characters in all the books were Swift's Glumdalclitch and Ernest Pontifex's spinster aunt Alethea in Samuel Butler's *The Way of All Flesh.*

themselves. I was, they said, older and more experienced than most, and I could not put my head on their shoulders.

I took their advice (anxious to please as always), and when I was impossibly bored, I read the curriculum materials that had been handed out earlier at Tougaloo. They were a revelation, for they specifically forbade "teaching" as I had until then understood it. Even the physical arrangement of the "classroom" was to be different from any I had ever sat in: no rows of chairs with the teacher at the front of the room; only "circles," with the teacher inside them. No "body of knowledge" that the teacher was to deliver to the students, but another procedure altogether: the teacher was to draw out of the students the knowledge of the world each of them lived in and the one they may have dreamed of; shared, this information could then be checked, through surveys or statistics, against the world beyond the church basement. Thus, for example, the question of inside plumbing: how many students described inside plumbing as they told about the houses they lived in, or those their mothers worked in? And according to surveys and statistical charts, who in Mississippi had and did not have inside plumbing in their houses?

The curriculum was organized to raise black students' consciousness of themselves as part of a separate "minority culture" that had its own identity, strengths, and weaknesses, its language and history, and that could decide its values and directions for the future. Thus, students attempted to define those aspects of their lives (the "minority culture") they wanted to keep and those they would change; in addition, they defined those aspects of the "majority culture" they would or would not want to adopt. In contemporary terms, we should describe the curriculum as interdisciplinary, problem solving, and very demanding. When we tried a unit on black history, for example, we tried to figure out whether Marcus Garvey's strategy was applicable in the 1960s. When it was clear that young black Mississippians looked to Chicago or New York rather than to Africa, we talked about why black people were "rioting" in those Northern cities. Even as we speculated, asked, and attempted to answer questions, we worked from a base of human experience—the knowledge these students had of black lives in Jackson, Mississippi.

As a teaching strategy, the curriculum was disarming for both teacher and students. Despite my age, race, and status, I could converse with teenage Mississippians in a manner that encouraged them to speak freely, in part because I did not have the information they did, and in part because my role had been defined differently from the traditional controlling teacherly one. If this was a "freedom school," my role as teacher was to create an environment in which students could decide to investigate this problem and not that, in which I was a resource but not an authority. Indeed, my authority was usefully bound, at least to help me learn a new role, by my whiteness and my visibility as a middle-class lady professor. I had no choice but to accept my differentness, and I learned that summer, through the creative writing of black students, that out of a sense of one's own identity can come rich expression and thought.

The teaching strategy is built on the assumption that the person who talks and who makes decisions about the direction of the conversation, or about what topic is to be investigated, learns; that talking is at least as important to learning as listening; and that, in a group, people can learn both to listen and to talk, whereas in a conventional classroom, the students learn to listen in order to memorize what the teacher has said. The strategy has two purposes: to break the hierarchical pattern that binds the traditional classroom (and in the case of a white teacher and black students, the hierarchy of race as well); and second, to encourage young blacks to understand that they have knowledge of value to themselves and to others. The strategy thus involves seeking out the knowledge and strengths people have, and building on them, rather than holding people up against a predetermined standard by which they must measure themselves (and find themselves wanting).

In the process of that summer I probably learned more than my students, especially about the politics of teaching.[12] At Goucher, that fall, I began to apply what I had learned, moving my chairs into a circle, asking questions that only students could answer, and attempting to find a curriculum that would meet the needs and interests of white, middle-class female students. Trying to learn how to teach women what eventually was called "consciousness" became the chief means of raising my own. Through most of the rest of the decade, I had to fight the hostility and suspicion of some students and faculty.

---

[12] And for the first time, I wrote an essay because I had something to say: see Howe (1965).

It is interesting to speculate about the refusal of faculty at a women's college to admit the legitimacy of devoting one whole course to women's lives. Even as late as 1970, I could not use the word "women" in the official description of the writing course I finally called "Identity and Expression" (Howe, 1971). By then I had demonstrated at least to my own satisfaction that good writing was the product of consciousness about one's personal and social identity, and that such consciousness could come out of a teacher's efforts to choose literature related to women's lives and to share her power in the classroom. Shared classroom power energizes and activates students and may turn them into leaders who wish to share their power with others—as well as into good writers.

Looking back, however, I can see that a social movement is helpful, if not essential, to the process. The civil rights movement in Mississippi provided a supportive context for change. Black students wanted to study black history and writers; they were interested in themselves and in comparing their lives to those of white students. They didn't need the motivation of grades, nor did they expect them in a "freedom" school. Goucher women, on the other hand, were defensive about being women: " 'Lady writers' were third-rate," one intrepid freshman said with some pique at finding herself holding my syllabus. She and others like her had no intention of talking about their lives: "Women were boring"—they wanted to read D. H. Lawrence and James Joyce. Thus, it is possible to understand the slowness with which women students took both to the strategy and to the curriculum: there was until 1969 no social context in which they and I could find support. On the contrary, they lived on a campus that valued only the most conservative paths for women, at a time in their lives when the pressures of peers and parents were harshest on them to conform, and when their own sexuality and that of Hopkins and Annapolis males were omnipresent. Thus, to ask them to assume the consciousness of their power as women was, at that moment in time, probably an unreasonable request.

And I, too, was slow to consider the potential power of an organized women's movement. I neither joined NOW nor interested myself in its work. Nor did I join a consciousness-raising group: I raised my consciousness, I continued to maintain, by teaching women. I had changed my life, and in the classroom, I would attempt to change students' lives. And I continued to deplore a "separatist" women's movement that had seemingly abandoned both the civil rights and the antiwar movements that seemed to me of primary consequence.

But in the spring of 1969, several women and I were appointed by the executive council of the Modern Language Association to a Commission on the Status of Women. Quite suddenly, I was not the individual teacher in a classroom, or even part of a band of volunteer teachers in Mississippi, but head of a group responsible for establishing "equity" for women in English and modern languages. I had, as Kate Millett used to say comically, arrived at the supreme position for women—the token. With other tokens in other professions, many of whom formed caucuses and were appointed to commissions during 1969 and 1970, we began the double task of charting the professional discrimination against women and raising their consciousness about their own condition.

Because of the Mississippi experience and my own decade of change, I emphasized, from the first, the importance of changing the education of women. Overt or simple discrimination was less than half of the problem. I knew from my own life and from the last five years of teaching women that most of the problems of inequity were more difficult to solve because of how they shaped what went on in women's heads. Thus, that was one place to begin. We had no word for it in 1969, but by 1970 women's studies had various labels. In the manner of the Mississippi Freedom Schools and the consciousness-raising group, and the experiments of my classroom, women's studies builds on the social reality of particular lives. Unlike traditional study, which begins from the standards of the "majority" class, race, and sex, as organized into "bodies of knowledge," this alternative process aims at developing consciousness about one's life in contrast or comparison to the norms that prevail. Organizing a process and curriculum called women's studies challenges traditional "bodies of knowledge" not only by replacing them (at least for a time), but more significantly by attempting to disestablish their authority. Consciousness about one's particular life and experience is the primary knowledge one needs not only to begin to investigate "bodies of knowledge," but to establish them in the first place. Thus, education becomes a key strategy to social change. As a singular movement, without organized head or agreed-upon strategy, women's studies has, nevertheless, begun a long and difficult task.

A 32-year-old mother of three children was explaining, as part of a panel on lifestyles, that when she and her husband were first married, she decided to use a small inheritance she had just received to send him to law school. "Why did you decide to do that with your money?" someone else on the panel asked. The student answered readily: "Because it was a good investment." And of course the class laughed. In response to the next question, "But why didn't *you* go to law school on that money?" she simply shrugged. There was no simple or comic answer to that question.

Listening to this interchange were 45 students in an introductory course in women's studies at the State University of New York/College at Old Westbury, in the fall of 1973. Their ages ranged, in an even spread, from 17 to 57; there were 5 males in the group, 8 black people, and several Puerto Rican women. The course was organized into five units of study:

1 The family and socialization, with special focus on mother/daughter or mother/son relationships

2 School and socialization

3 Adolescence and sexuality

4 Choices: Marriage and other lifestyles; college or work; career, vocation

5 Feminism and the future

Students were aware of two goals the teacher projected for the course: to raise the consciousness of the participants and to add measurably to their knowledge about the maturation of women and men. Texts included short stories and other literature of experience, essays, and research studies written by social scientists, as well as statistical graphs and charts and some historical material. Students were expected to keep a journal reflecting both their experience of the two 90-minute classroom sessions

[13] I wish to acknowledge the assistance of a grant (1971–1973) from the National Endowment for the Humanities (RO–5085–72–54) in gathering information for this section.

and two reading assignments each week. The journal was to record their intellectual and emotional growth through the semester. Students were also expected to complete a group project of an investigatory nature. While the diversity of this particular group of students may not be typical, the curriculum taught, the teaching strategies, and the goals of the course are characteristic of a new national educational movement.

The thrust of this movement has been to change the education primarily of women, though men have been involved from the first, both as teachers and as students.[14] The major instrument has been the sharing of knowledge, resources, and teaching methods through the development of a network that has published bibliographies of courses and programs; syllabi, reading lists, and essays about teaching women's studies; and more recently, the *Women's Studies Newsletter.* To share knowledge is, as I have made clear earlier, to allow for the development of many leaders, and thus for the rapid spread of a political movement.

Women's studies began informally on approximately 47 campuses with the initiation usually of a single course in the academic year 1969–70.[15] I say "informally," since there had been no prior discussion or planning, and few of those pioneers in curriculum change had been in touch with each other before the late fall of 1970. During the previous spring, Sheila Tobias and I—in two separate places—began to receive course syllabi and reading lists from teachers of women's studies courses and requests from others who wanted to begin such courses. In each case, the correspondence that accompanied the syllabi or requests assumed, naturally, that women were willing to share such materials. Totally absent was the conventional paranoia that fosters academic secrecy, even about reading lists. In the main, early courses were taught by junior faculty and graduate students at such prestigious institutions as Cornell, Wesleyan, Stanford, Yale, Princeton, Smith, and Barnard, as well as at

[14] From the first, about 10 percent of students and faculty have been males. Of late, a number of teachers have reported that up to 20 percent of their students are male.

[15] A more elaborate history of women's studies, and its relationship particularly to the free university movement of the sixties, is to be found in Howe and Ahlum, "Women's Studies and Social Change" (1973).

Douglass, San Diego State, American University, the University of Pittsburgh, and the College of St. Catherine in St. Paul, Minnesota.[16]

In the fall of 1970, Ms. Tobias published 17 course syllabi, all but one in history, the social sciences, and "interdisciplinary" areas, under the rubric *Female Studies;* she was especially foresightful to call the volume "No. 1." In December 1970, under the aegis of the Modern Language Association's Commission on the Status of Women, *Female Studies II* offered 66 syllabi and reading lists, 30 of which were in literature, the remainder in history, social science, and "interdisciplinary" areas. Both volumes and those that followed (the ninth and tenth volumes of the series will appear in 1975) provided a growing group of interested teacher-scholars not only with ideas and resources, but also with some political clout: If Harvard, Princeton, Smith, Yale, and Barnard could offer women's studies courses, why not the University of Pennsylvania or Indiana? If San Diego State, why not Long Beach, or Sacramento, or any of the other California campuses? A little less than four years later, one can list over 4,600 courses that have been offered in women's studies, approximately 2,500 of which were offered during the academic year 1973–74.[17]

Courses have developed in every area of university study, though there are still relatively few in the hard sciences, and more in literature, history, and sociology, or in interdisciplinary combinations of these, than in all the other disciplines combined. There are also more courses in law than in other graduate or professional schools. Whatever the course, however, two or three patterns are significant. First, the rediscovery of nineteenth-century history and literature runs throughout the curriculum, regardless of the disciplinary origin or title of the

---

[16] While most of the early courses seemed to come from institutions on the East Coast, this was a phase of Eastern chauvinism, corrected the following year with a broadening of the communications network. See listings as of summer 1973 in Ahlum and Howe (1971, 1972) and Miller, Fitzmaurice, Berkowitz, and Ahlum (1973).

[17] A grant from the Ford Foundation has helped to survey the academic world and to produce *Who's Who and Where in Women's Studies* (Tamar Berkowitz, Jean Mangi and Jane Williamson, eds.), scheduled for late 1974, The Feminist Press, Old Westbury, New York.

course. Thus, in speech, courses focus on the "rhetoric" of nineteenth-century feminists, either alone or in contrast to their twentieth-century counterparts. A singular course in journalism also takes a historical perspective and rediscovers feminist journalists of the nineteenth century. Courses in economics or politics, as well as in sociology, are sometimes difficult to distinguish from courses in history. Similarly, many social science and history courses depend for materials on newly recovered or discovered autobiographies, memoirs, diaries, letters, or other writings of nineteenth-century women. Stories by such writers as Mary Wilkins Freeman and Rebecca Harding Davis are used in both history and literature courses. Indeed, the interdisciplinary nature of most women's studies courses makes disciplinary identification sometimes nothing more than a function of the title or the department from which a course derives.

As significant as the interest in nineteenth-century feminist history and literature is another in sociological and psychological implications of sex-role development. No literature or history course, no art history or philosophy course begins without defining sex roles as learned, not innate. Introductory courses are often devoted to aspects of socialization, and more advanced courses in the social sciences to new research in this area or to cross-cultural studies.

One additional curricular pattern is the emphasis on the future. If students begin to understand that they have a history, and if they also understand that sex roles are developed, not innate, they may naturally begin to think about change. Thus, many teachers' designs include codas on the future: What kinds of marriage contracts will partners write in 1980? What kinds of child-care centers should be instituted? How could housework be industrialized? How does an idea become implemented? Of what use is the passage of a law forbidding discrimination on the basis of sex? Answers to such questions insist upon the students' knowing the past as well as the present, but putting such knowledge to work for the future.

Three teaching strategies are as politically significant as the curricular items I have just mentioned. They are responses to and adaptations of the movement's consciousness-raising groups, and an emphasis on "sisterhood" and on action. With a trained student leader, the small group functions cooperatively rather than competitively. It is not a place where one advances one's own grade: for one thing, the teacher is rarely present. It is, rather, a place in which one learns to work with others, either to learn from their experience or their understanding of the material under discussion or to make a contribution to the group. In addition, groups often function as vehicles for term projects or papers. Group grades are not uncommon in this instance, and part of the learning process is the experience of dealing with those problems that group research raises: distributing labor equally; making use of various kinds of talents and resources; encouraging the shy to participate and the domineering to relax. Obviously, such projects require skilled leadership, and the teacher's job is to provide that by training a group of students to lead such activities.

The action project that substitutes for the library paper is also a commonplace of women's studies courses. While this activity is related to such innovations as field studies or internships, established in many institutions since the sixties, in a women's studies program it is likely to be related to the women's movement, or to women's needs on or off the campus. In law courses, for example, students take on research for actual cases as aides to lawyers or they attempt to rewrite legislation in connection with the work of an interested legislator. Other women are engaged in community health projects, or in counseling, or in developing nonsexist curricula for public schools. At California State College/Sonoma, students in a women's studies course began to collect information about forgotten or neglected women artists, made slides of their work, built up a collection about some 200 artists, and have shown the slide show at high schools in their area and colleges across the country.

Such work is obviously useful, even as it is academically impeccable. It is also politically potent, since it both satisfies the needs of the women's movement and, in the process, trains future leaders of that movement. Leaders are trained not only through the development of their skills, consciousness, and knowledge, but through the successful application of these in the course of their education.

One additional teaching strategy deserves special attention. I leave for last the journal writing that fills most women's studies courses because it has not usually been understood as a political tool. Most students are required to keep journals at least in introductory courses, and often in others as well. Usually, instructions call for the student to reflect on the experiences she encounters in the course and especially on the reading, talking, and thinking she has been provoked to. The journal functions, in many courses, as an alternative to traditional examinations, and allows students to develop their own program of learning, even as they choose to comment on particular matters of significance. Thus, journal entries become a means through which students develop and record their own growing political awareness. As a composition teacher of some 20 years, moreover, I suspect that the act of writing it down is more indelible than the acts of thinking or speaking the same message. The need to write it down may also force more organized thinking. Interestingly, even those students who complain about the requirement usually confess, by the end of the semester, that they have found the journal useful for their own development. Students often report continuing a journal through other courses, though they may not be fulfilling a requirement. I consider the journal as potent a political tool as the activist group project, for it fosters confidence in a necessary skill, as well as the significant growth of consciousness about one's own and others' lives.

As the educational arm of the women's movement, women's studies has three particular tasks to accomplish, the first two of which are clearly under way. In an institutional setting that has been traditionally careless of or hostile to women, the women's studies teacher has led the development of courses and teaching strategies aimed at changing the consciousness of women (and men), and at adding new knowledge to their ken. Equipped thus with consciousness and knowledge, their students have brought fresh leadership to ongoing movements for change on campus and off. Second, both teachers and students have added significantly to areas of knowledge and new research developments in such fields as sex-role socialization and gender identity. The history of women, and literature by and about women, have spawned in the past several years an extraordinary series of publications, including three new scholarly journals and a host of "special issues" of established ones, several hundred books, and scores of bibliographies. While there is but one doctoral program in women's studies (at SUNY/Binghamton in women's history), the effect of the movement on dissertation topics is considerable.[18]

The third task, dependent on the first two, is more elusive: to change the male-centered college curriculum, with regard not only to women generally, but to women of various classes and races. The readiness of higher education for such change cannot be judged by the massive proliferation of women's studies courses and programs, since it is always easier to add to the college curriculum than to change it in any substantive way. To change the curriculum would be to change those teaching it: not only to affect their consciousness about the need for such changes, but to add to their knowledge. It is not simply that women should be added to the history curriculum: rather, a study of women's role in the development of the frontier, for example, or on the plantation during the Civil War, changes the conception of those historical periods. It is not simply that women artists have been omitted from the curriculum: we have taught students to believe that there were none. Admitting that error, reviewing the work, for example, of anonymous female artists as well as of those whose names are known, necessitates a review of aesthetic criteria on which admission to the canon of art history has been based. It is not simply that women receive no attention in child development or developmental psychology courses: it is that male development is taught as though it were generic. Revision of such curriculum is not a matter of scissors and paste, but of significant, holistic change. To accomplish such change, an institution would have to invest in consciousness-raising workshops or courses for its faculty; professors would have to read in and begin research on areas new to them; and both the administration and the faculty would have to value women students—and new knowledge, generally—sufficiently to turn their attention to these goals.

While it is far too early to utter predictions about women's studies' efficacy in attempting to change college curriculum, it is possible to explore the political levers and strategies for such change. Quite early in the movement, teachers and students

[18] Three hundred in 1973 and four hundred in 1974 applied for Ford Foundation's Doctoral Dissertation Fellowships in Women's Studies (administered in 1974 by the Woodrow Wilson Foundation). It is interesting to note that, of the 27 awarded in 1974, 11 were in history and 11 others in social science.

came together to form "programs," though not usually for the purpose of accreditation via the granting of degrees or the establishment of "minors." Unlike individual courses, a women's studies program is an administrative unit, with a designated "coordinator" or "committee" to carry out its function.

Thus identified, women's studies programs in 1971, when there were approximately 17, issued manifesto-like statements of intent and strategy. Often, these aimed at both gaining administrative support and recruiting students. Included were the needs to raise the consciousness of women about themselves and their history and to compensate for the omission of women from the traditional curriculum. Some programs also announced their intention of working toward the discovery of feminist history and culture; others called for the support of new research. While all were obviously interested in changing the education of women, several programs openly called also for the need to change the ongoing curriculum of the university (Howe & Ahlum, 1971; Rosenfelt, 1973).

As an *indirect* effort to change higher education for women, women's studies programs can be viewed as functioning in the manner of parallel institutions. Indeed, program offerings may look like mini-college catalogs—a smorgasbord of courses from many traditional "departments" or "disciplines," plus some novel and usually interdisciplinary ones. Parallel institutions rarely change their hosts directly, though they often produce leadership that may affect other institutions. Thus, while the Mississippi Freedom Schools did not change education for black students in Mississippi, the movement trained hundreds of Northern college students and teachers who put their new knowledge of leadership and teaching strategies to work in their home institutions. Similarly, the free universities that proliferated in the mid-sixties did not change the institutions they were peripherally attached to. Rather, many of those students and particularly some of those teachers who functioned in the free universities took their new skills, consciousness, and knowledge and put them to work in traditional institutions.

This view of women's studies programs as parallel institutions anticipates their development as separate units within a given institution. From the beginning, however, perhaps forewarned by the experiences of black studies, women's studies leaders have sought institutional forms other than simple separatism.

Thus, programs were thought of as interdepartmental or as "networks" rather than as traditional departments. In a number of institutions, women's studies has developed through the efforts of faculty who divide their time between traditional departments and women's studies. In some institutions, the Universities of Delaware, Pittsburgh, and Washington, for example, new appointments in women's studies are contingent on the agreement of traditional departments. The political perspective behind such ambiguous forms of organization is that of change: rather than be cut off, or separated from, the centers of university life in traditional departments, women's studies leaders have attempted to straddle both worlds.

For many, this has become an increasingly frustrating experience. In a nondepartmental world of women's studies, who is responsible for gaining office space, a budget, faculty lines, a library, and other resources for students? In some institutions, a friendly divisional dean or an umbrella of interdisciplinary programs has been the helpful vehicle, but obviously funds must be shared among a proliferating number of interdisciplinary areas of study. And so, women's studies programs may turn in the direction of more formalized departmental structures. While I am sympathetic to the weariness of women who have worked for years without that departmental secretary, budget, and office, and without the power to hire and fire, I am also concerned lest a potent strategy for change harden into a new kind of ghetto for women.

The test of women's studies on campus will not finally be the proliferation of courses or programs, but their effect on the rest of the curriculum. If by 1980, the number of courses and programs has doubled or tripled, and if in freshman English the students are still reading male writers on male lives, and in United States history the students are still studying male-culture heroes, wars, and male political documents, then we shall have failed our mission.

From the beginning, there has been still another mission for women's studies: to assist the reeducation of women outside the conventional undergraduate population. The extension of women's studies into women's centers, continuing education programs, schools of education, nursing, and social work, and into inservice education programs for teachers, is a development of the last 18 months.[19] In addition, there have been several hundred attempts to introduce women's studies courses, especially in English and history, into the high school curriculum; and at least one school system, Berkeley, is attempting to develop a women's studies curriculum (especially geared for a racially mixed population) in its elementary schools. Such developments are extraordinarily significant, for they suggest the ability of women's studies to affect the great mass of women outside the college population.

STRATEGIES AND CONCLUSIONS While women's studies as an addition to the campus is, of course, a lively reality, the test of its power to change the education of women has hardly begun. All that has been accomplished, moreover, has occurred without the benefit of national organization or strategic planning by those involved in the women's studies movement. While there are women's caucuses or official commissions in nearly every professional association by now, representatives of these groups have met together only rarely and briefly. The Professional Women's Caucus, an effort to unite women from the trade union movement with those from academe and other professions, has not, for obvious reasons, been able to focus on academic women alone. More recently still, a coalition of professional associations, caucuses, commissions, and other feminist organizations was brought together under a national umbrella. The National Federation of Women's Professional Groups will publish a newsletter and provide informational resources to groups that join. Like the Clearinghouse on Women's Studies itself, none of these efforts establishes more than a network. While networks are an indispensable prelude to national organization, they cannot substitute indefinitely for that organization itself. Without an

---

[19] During the 1973–74 academic year, in at least two places (Old Westbury, New York, and Seattle, Washington) women's studies faculty and local school systems have begun cooperatively to develop women's studies courses for an inservice education curriculum. Such courses raise the consciousness of teachers, provide them with new knowledge, and assist them in developing strategies for incorporating their learning into the ongoing curriculum. It is, again, too early to predict developments here, but conferences planned for the fall and winter of 1974 should push this movement into national prominence.

organization the work of strategic planning will be left to others, including such groups as the Carnegie Commission on Higher Education.

The Carnegie report *Opportunities for Women in Higher Education* (1973) is subtitled "Their Current Participation, Prospects for the Future, and Recommendations for Action." Because I believe that the report is an important one—it may even be an influential one—I shall analyze and comment on the vision of its authors and, where relevant, offer an alternative view.[20]

The first function of the authors, to define the "various barriers that have existed in the paths of women" (p. 165), is managed with tact. "Academic recruitment procedures," for example, are described as "tend[ing] to be somewhat 'cosy.'" "Especially among the more prestigious departments," the authors continue, "openings are not publicized" (p. 120). While the "barriers" to the equitable employment and advancement of academic women are not explicated as fully or as strongly as in *Academic Women on the Move* (Rossi & Calderwood, 1973), it is impossible to avoid a similar conclusion: the academic world is responsible and restitution is certainly in order. In addition, the authors offer a briefer view of the more basic problem: the aspirations of women, as affected by family, school, and society generally, even before admission to college. They are to be commended for paying close attention to the differences in opportunity afforded working-class and middle-class women. Further, the authors report on "evidence of discrimination in undergraduate admissions," and note the need for assembling documentation of a still more complex variety of discrimination against women graduate students.[21] The tone throughout is

[20] While the report is issued, like others in the series, under the joint responsibility of a prestigious panel of 16 men and 2 women (Patricia Roberts Harris and Katherine E. McBride), acknowledgments include the names of four staff members, presumably the text's writers and researchers (Margaret S. Gordon, Elizabeth Scott, Laura Kent, and Jane McClosky), as well as a roster of a dozen academic and foundation women (and one man), many of them prominent feminists, who read and commented on drafts. Such contributions by individuals, like the book this essay is a part of, cannot be viewed as substitutes for the ongoing discussions of the Carnegie Commission itself during the last half-dozen years, much less for national organization and debate among academic women.

[21] "There also remains the possibility that faculty members in leading research universities, who tend not only to be overwhelmingly male but also to have prestigious reputations, are more likely to discourage women from entering their

judicious: a balanced presentation of academic culpability accompanied by numerous guidelines for change. Taken as a whole, however, the net effect of the volume is not auspicious for academic women, nor for young women just entering school this year. While the authors are not to be blamed for reporting the depressing realities of the academic world as it currently exists, they may be criticized for softening that reality, especially with regard to the next 30 years.

The prognosis appears refrain-like throughout the latter half of the volume: "These changes will come slowly . . ." and for two reasons. The first of these may be shocking to those who do not know recent academic history: ". . . during the decade of the most explosive growth in the history of higher education—the 1960s—women lost ground as a percentage of members of regular faculty ranks in four-year institutions, especially at the associate professor level, and gained ground only at the instructor level" (p. 110).[22] At least once the authors allow themselves a plaintive sentence, as they declare that, "As in the case of graduate students, it would have been far easier to provide increased opportunities for women on faculties a decade ago, when enrollments were rising exceedingly rapidly" (p. 125). And they note also as "surprising" the fact that "both the relative representation and status of women have deteriorated over the last 50 years" (pp. 111–112). Thus, one can only conclude that, left to its own devices, the academic world would only continue its neglect of women (and minority groups).

But the depressing prognosis depends as well on the additional fact that while some institutional growth will occur in the 1970s, there will be little or none in the following decade, and nothing for many decades to come (if ever) to match the 1960s. Since women, in effect, lost ground on faculties and in administrations through the decade of the 1960s, and since the growth rate of the

fields than are faculty members in comprehensive colleges and liberal arts colleges. There is some evidence that this tendency is not confined to traditionally male fields" (p. 68). The tone is characteristic of the report.

[22] Women lost ground, though not so dramatically, also at the full professor and assistant professor levels. The general percentage of women on four-year college faculties declined from 19.1 percent in 1959–60 to 19.0 percent in 1971–72, during a decade when some institutions doubled their enrollments and new ones opened their doors for the first time.

education industry is slowing and will presumably come to a halt by 1980, it will take considerable time for women to "catch up" to where they should be, even according to their current numbers and proportions in various disciplines. The best that can be hoped for, therefore, is to maintain the status quo in female-typed fields and to add a few women to male-typed fields. If *half* of all new faculty hired henceforth were women, by 1990 30 percent of faculties would be female. Not sanguine about that possibility, the authors of the Carnegie report try another prediction, and suggest that perhaps by the year 2000 women will be "included in the national professoriate in approximately the same proportions as they are in the total labor force." They urge solemnly that "this is a task for a generation of effort" (p. 6).

Behind these predictions lies an estimate that allows for the doubling of the percentage of women who earn the doctorate annually—to 30 percent; and a hope that these 30 percent will, in the course of the next 30 years, fill 30 percent of the faculty slots in four-year institutions. That is a modest enough goal. And as depressing as it may seem for people who want to see change occur more quickly, it is an optimistic view, given the specific projections (printed in the Appendix) for the next two to five years by Harvard, Stanford, and Columbia.[23]

Hence, one is left with an equivocal impression: on the one hand, the report is forthright and unflinching in its view of discrimination against women, and it prescribes a number of specific strategies to repair the damage—affirmative action, improved high school counseling, women's studies, part-time flexibility, child-care services, etc.; but on the other hand, change is bound to be slow, and the supporting details of the Appendix make that change likely to be slower still.

In light of the prognosis, two strategies emerge from the Carnegie report. The most obvious of these is the emphasis on affirmative action guidelines and goals. The authors make an effort here to reassure male critics of affirmative action that "colleges and universities can achieve affirmative action goals

---

[23] If one compares the general hope—to achieve faculties on which 30 percent are women—with the plans of Harvard, Stanford, and Columbia, one can only conclude that *other,* less prestigious institutions (and women's colleges—which the authors encourage to continue) will make up for their deficiencies. Such dual standards will simply continue things as they are.

without the lowering of standards . . ." (p. 137). Their own rationale hinges on the key word "balance," as though that might appeal to departments hitherto and for a hundred years or more, presumably, "unbalanced" in their rosters of white male scholars. Despite the evidence of the 1960s, the authors emphasize voluntary compliance, a function no doubt of Carnegie's general distaste for the hand of the federal government in higher education, and a preference for more indirect methods of control. Whether one espouses direct or indirect methods, some means of enforcement beyond morality and goodwill are essential, especially since they have not been effective motivators of change in the past, or even in recent history. In their concluding remarks, the authors resort to optimism, suggesting the need only for "interim" "federal pressure for affirmative action and pressure from campus and professional women's groups," and hoping that "as attitudes change, aspirations of women toward participation in higher education on a basis of equal opportunity with men will come to be taken for granted" (p. 165).

A second major strategy is more daring and progressive: it is based on recent analyses of an increasingly sex-typed academic and professional world, and projects the encouragement of women to enter "nontraditional" fields. Certainly many feminists would applaud this aim, since a major principle of the women's movement has called for integrating the work force. If I am dubious about the principle, it is that such integration has not been of particular benefit to women. Quite the reverse: Caroline Bird describes, for example, the integration of males into library schools that resulted in their rapid assumption of major administrative responsibilities in the largest, most prestigious libraries, where they were often trained by women (Bird, 1968). We all know how deferentially males are treated when they enter such female work worlds as nursing or elementary education. For the young male kindergarten teacher, the pipelines are greased on the route to administrative jobs. For women, we know that integration has usually meant a place at the bottom as in the feminization of the bank teller's job, or the teaching profession itself.

What would it mean for women to enter nontraditional fields? Given the technological world of the late twentieth century, it would obviously be desirable for women to become true participants in science and related professions. But the issue of "true" participation gives me pause, especially when I consider the relationship between numbers and power. With the statistics projected by the Carnegie report, it is inconceivable that women entering nontraditional fields could, by 2000, be any more, still, than "tokens." Even if the percentage of women engineers or architects increased from the current 1 percent to 6, they should still be tokens. Indeed, the writers of the Carnegie report use this fact to comfort "white male academic critics" who "exaggerate the threat to employment opportunities for white men."

Granted we are facing a situation in which the rate of increase in the number of faculty members employed is slowing down, and faculty employment may well become stationary or actually decline for a time in the 1980s. The potential job shortage for both sexes is most serious in the humanities and arts, in which women tend to be relatively well represented, but there are so few female Ph.D.'s in some of the traditionally male fields that it will be a long time before the competition of women presents any real threat (p. 139).

Not only would there be no possibility for developing feminist leadership in those traditional male professions; there would be no base sizable enough from which to organize for change. With all that said, however, it is still possible to encourage women to enter nontraditional fields—for other, more long-range reasons—but only as one part of a two-pronged strategy.

The second prong seems to me both of more immediate and of more ultimate consequence. Instead of bemoaning the fact that women numerically dominate the teaching, nursing, and social work professions, why not consider that fact important strategically? Why encourage the most talented women to enter a physics laboratory rather than a school superintendent's office or a department of educational administration? Why is it more important to spread a thin tokendom of women through the nontraditional kingdoms than to attempt a transformation of the traditional ghettos themselves—especially if one of those, the public school system, is responsible for the perpetuation of sex stereotyping and the low aspirations of women? It is here that I would want to move the writers of the Carnegie report, again, one step further. In the Carnegie report, women emerge as victims of both discrimination and socialization, but not as potential agents of their own change, much less agents of social change more generally. Since numbers are obviously useful both for building a base of support for change and for providing a large pool of talent from which to draw leaders, I would concentrate major energies during the next decade on the female professions, especially public school teaching. If schools are the major social agency responsible for socialization of the young, and if these schools are populated mainly with women, themselves socialized to do the job, clearly it is essential to release those teachers from the treadmill. The process needed is one similar to that invented by teachers of women's studies: new teaching strategies and a curriculum that builds on the lives and experiences of those studying.

I do not mean to suggest that by substituting female for male principals of elementary schools that the stereotypic treatment of girls and boys in classrooms will automatically halt, or that by replacing men with women in the hierarchy we shall change the structure and process of that hierarchy. But each year that I have traveled, I have met intrepid feminist teachers, leaving or in the process of making plans to leave public education—either for law school or for a Ph.D. program, and often with a special interest in women's studies. Some of these women could have offered an alternative vision to traditional leadership, but to none of them had such a possibility occurred. I would like to put such thoughts into feminists' heads, and to see programs begun expressly designed for new leadership. The next decade may be especially crucial if, as males enter to integrate the female job world, energetic feminists leave to seek careers elsewhere.

But more than leadership is needed to change the professions dominated by women. The service professions, like housework and child care, have always been held in low esteem both by the male world and by women themselves. And yet, of course, a complex society like this one could not continue to function without such work. To teach children, to serve the sick, the troubled, and the needy—these are significant tasks. How they are accomplished has been decided not by the women who do these daily jobs, but by males sometimes far from that place of work in both space and time. A consciousness about the potential of "womanpower," a knowledge of women's use of power, and an analysis of the current work and status of public school teachers, nurses, and social workers might lead, as in the case of nurses recently, to an awareness that the job needs redefinition by the workers themselves. What if a school or system's elementary school teachers told their (male) administration and school board (and their male-dominated union) that they wanted to redefine the curriculum? One could not imagine a more desirable, less painful means of implementing the federal guidelines to Title IX than to educate skilled new feminist leadership and huge numbers of informed and conscious teachers. We should not need to enforce Title IX on physical education: teachers might decide for themselves that both girls and boys need sound and integrated programs from grade one forward.

The question of timing deserves a special note. In part because they have been ghettos for women, in part because feminists have tended to shun the traditionally female, these professions have been the last to feel the impact of the women's movement: they need the interest and support of feminists to encourage those initiatives already under way. From women's caucuses and programs in teachers' unions, for example, have come a variety of conferences and publications on the subject of sex-role stereotyping, and there is now a useful center functioning in Washington to promote continued efforts.[24]

At the beginning of this essay, I asked several questions about breaking away from the control of a male-centered world without assuming its guises and reversing its patriarchy, without extending new forms of oppression to other women, to groups of minorities, or to men themselves. One early strategy depended on the somewhat ostrich-like assumption that women could cultivate their own sphere, assume power over their own lives, without affecting men's. When that first wave of nineteenth-century feminism impinged on males, it was to ask for "equality" in the male world, without changing its essential maleness. The recent movement has also built on similar assumptions about women seizing power over their own lives, but the methods have been more self-consciously in opposition to patriarchy's own: "sisterhood" and the sharing of power aim deliberately to undercut traditional authority. How profound is this movement for change? Not the last five years but the next ten will begin to tell us.

---

[24] The Resource Center on Sex Roles in Education, a project of the National Foundation for the Improvement of Education.

CONCLUSION In the beginning of this book, I note that the "chief effect of the women's movement on higher education" has been its "impact on the lives of academic women." No doubt this effect will continue to be felt among new generations now in schools or colleges: increasing numbers of women will be motivated to organize their lives around careers and egalitarian relationships, and many of these women will choose nontraditional careers. But even optimists declare that the numbers of women entering such professions as medicine, engineering, and architecture will remain minuscule unless three coordinated efforts begin: at the elementary school level, where girls are not expected to succeed at mathematics and science; at the high school and college levels, where girls are discouraged from pursuing studies in science and technology; and in the professions themselves, where the "old boys' clubs" remain untouched by the past decade of the women's movement. In those nontraditional areas, the battle to be fought still is for entrance, not for equity or power. It will be several decades before women's caucuses can make significant changes in any facet of those professions.

But there is another and more immediate effort possible: the power of women to change traditionally female professions. It is not that I urge women to keep their "place." Indeed, I expect and encourage a perceptible shift of women toward the nontraditional professions. But at the same time, I am concerned about such professions as nursing, social work, and teaching, their esteem now demeaned by two labels—"female" and "traditional." In the current decade and in the next, I should like to see feminist energies in higher education focused on these areas.

If the strategy I suggest as most important for those next ten years seems to come full circle—to urge the development of women's power in those areas where they are most numerous— teaching, nursing, social work—it is not because I think of these as belonging only to women. They are critical for the lives of men and children as well as women. To focus feminist energies on them now would be to develop "womanpower" to change three of the most important service institutions in the society. Academic women have used this first decade to change their own lives; the next one will tell us whether those changes contain the power to alter the institutions in which they and large numbers of their students work.

REFERENCES

Ahlum, Carol, and Florence Howe: *The New Guide to Female Studies,* no. 1, KNOW, Inc., Pittsburgh, 1971.

Ahlum, Carol, and Florence Howe: *The New Guide to Female Studies,* no. 2, The Feminist Press, Old Westbury, N.Y., 1972.

Bardwick, Judith M.: *Psychology of Women,* Harper & Row, Publishers, Incorporated, New York, 1971.

Bird, Caroline: *Born Female,* David McKay Company, Inc., New York, 1968.

Carden, Maren Lockwood: *The New Feminist Movement,* Russell Sage Foundation, New York, 1974.

Carnegie Commission on Higher Education: *Opportunities for Women in Higher Education,* McGraw-Hill Book Company, New York, 1973.

Clark, Burton R.: "The 'Cooling-Out' Function in Higher Education," *American Journal of Sociology,* vol. 65, pp. 569–576, May 1960.

Fuller, Margaret: *Woman in the Nineteenth Century,* W. W. Norton & Company, Inc., New York, 1971.

Horner, Matina S.: "Fail, Bright Women," *Psychology Today,* vol. 3, no. 6, pp. 36–38, November 1969.

Howe, Florence: "Mississippi's Freedom Schools: The Politics of Education," *Harvard Educational Review,* vol. 35, pp. 144–160, Spring 1965.

Howe, Florence: *Female Studies II,* KNOW, Inc., Pittsburgh, 1970.

Howe, Florence: "Identity and Expression: A Writing Course for Women," *College English,* vol. 32, pp. 863–871, May 1971.

Howe, Florence, and Carol Ahlum: *Female Studies III,* KNOW, Inc., Pittsburgh, 1971.

Howe, Florence, and Carol Ahlum: "Women's Studies and Social Change," in Alice S. Rossi and Ann Calderwood (eds.), *Academic Women on the Move,* Russell Sage Foundation, New York, 1973.

Howe, Florence, John McClusky, and Elizabeth Wilson: "Hierarchy, Power, and Women in Educational Policy Making," unpublished essay.

McClelland, D. C., J. Atkinson, R. Clark, and E. Lowell: *The Achievement Motive,* Appleton & Company, Inc., New York, 1953.

McClusky, John: "Beyond the Carrot and the Stick: Liberation and Power without Control," unpublished essay. Also "Adult Models' Liberating and Debilitating Influence on Young Women in the U.S. Educational System," an unpublished project proposal.

Miller, Joanna, Michelina Fitzmaurice, Tamar Berkowitz, and Carol Ahlum: *The New Guide to Female Studies,* no. 3, The Feminist Press, Old Westbury, N.Y., 1973.

Mitchell, Juliet: *Women's Estate,* Pantheon Books, New York, 1971.

Rosenfelt, Deborah Silverton: *Female Studies VII: Going Strong,* The Feminist Press, Old Westbury, N.Y., 1973.

Rossi, Alice S. (ed.): *The Feminist Papers,* Columbia University Press, New York, 1973.

Rossi, Alice S. (ed.): *Essays on Sex Equality,* The University of Chicago Press, Chicago, 1970.

Rossi, Alice S., and Ann Calderwood (eds.): *Academic Women on the Move,* Russell Sage Foundation, New York, 1973.

Showalter, Elaine: "Women and the Literary Curriculum," *College English,* vol. 32, pp. 855–862, May 1971.

Tobias, Sheila: *Female Studies I,* KNOW, Inc., Pittsburgh, 1970.

Wollstonecraft, Mary: *A Vindication of the Rights of Woman,* W. W. Norton & Company, Inc., New York, 1967.

Index